W9-BZZ-601

LIBRARY
NASH COMMUNITY COLLEGE
P. O. BOX 7488
ROCKY MOUNT, N. C. 27804

CZECH REPUBLIC

CZECH REPUBLIC

BY PETRA PRESS

LUCENT BOOKS
P.O. BOX 289011
SAN DIEGO, CA 92198-9011

Library of Congress Cataloging-in-Publication Data

Press, Petra.
  Czech Republic / by Petra Press.
     p. cm. — (Modern nations of the world)
  Includes bibliographical references and index.
  ISBN 1-56006-759-4 (alk. paper)
  1. Czech Republic—Juvenile literature. I. Title. II. Series.
  DB2011 .P744 2001
  943.71—dc21

                                            00-010222

No part of this book may be reproduced or used in any form or by any means, electrical, mechanical, or otherwise, including, but not limited to, photocopy, recording, or any information storage and retrieval system, without prior written permission from the publisher.

Copyright © 2002 by Lucent Books, Inc.
P.O. Box 289011, San Diego, CA 92198-9011
Printed in the U.S.A.

CONTENTS

INTRODUCTION

A COUNTRY OF CONTRASTS

The Czech Republic is a land of fairy-tale beauty, located in almost the exact center of the continent of Europe. Its rugged snowcapped mountains, rolling plains, and lush river valleys make it one of the more beautiful countries in Europe, yet its history is filled with ugly, bloody battles against neighboring tyrants who have tried to dominate it over the centuries.

The Czech Republic is a country of interesting contrasts. The Republic itself is a new nation, little more than a decade old, yet Czech history dates back thousands of years. In the last decade, thousands of tourists have poured across the country's newly opened borders to enjoy its rich heritage of art and music, while Czechs themselves rush to embrace Western technology and pop culture. The stunning urban landscape featuring architecture of ancient castles and cathedrals is marred by the filth of air pollution, the snarls of traffic congestion, and the presence of rising crime. The country has some of the richest, most fertile farmland in all of Europe, yet people in its rural areas struggled for almost a half century under Communist totalitarianism to eke out a minimal standard of living, and they have a long way to go to catch up.

Czechs are a primarily Slavic people who take pride that their unique identity has never been extinguished over the centuries despite the country's many occupiers, which include Hungary, Austria, Germany, and the Soviet Union. The peace-loving Czechs endured particularly horrific treatment under Nazi occupation and Soviet totalitarianism in the twentieth century. Perhaps that is why they continue to protest loudly against the world's practicing dictatorships and take an active role in United Nations (UN) peacekeeping missions. Yet in spite of the diverse ethnic influences that have contributed to their unique identity and the persecution they have had to endure as minorities in other empires, Czechs do not always appreciate the cultural diversity of minorities within their own borders, and they have been criticized by international humanitarian groups for their own racial discrimination.

But perhaps their most admirable national trait is that Czechs are survivors. They are dedicated to modernizing their country's long-outdated transportation and communications systems so they can join international trade and security organizations such as the European Union (EU) and North Atlantic Treaty Organization (NATO). The government is offering incentives to foreign investors to boost the growing economy. Art, music, and literature that became stagnant under Communist censorship are once again thriving. Businesses, farms, banks, and industries that were once government owned and managed are now almost all privately owned. Free-market competition has finally stimulated the economy. Unemployment rates are going down and construction is booming.

Learning to thrive in a whole new kind of economy is only one of the challenges facing the Czech people. Getting legislators in a multiparty democracy to agree on all the necessary economic and political reforms can be frustratingly slow. How can a small nation like the Czech Republic remain separate and independent when its economy depends on world trade and its security depends on strong international alliances? How can environmental protection regulations be implemented without putting struggling industries out of business and causing energy costs to skyrocket? How can hate crimes and racial discrimination be prevented without infringing on freedom of speech? Those are just some of the questions legislators debate every day.

Although the challenges are great, it is an exciting time for Czechs. After centuries of domination by others, they are finally controlling their own destinies.

1

GEOGRAPHY

The Czech Republic is a small landlocked European country bordering Germany, Austria, Slovakia, and Poland. The Česká Republika, as it is known in the Czech language, is almost exactly in the geographic center of Europe, which has made it a crossroads of culture and trade for more than fifteen centuries.

Despite its status as a crossroads, the nation's forests and mountains provide natural boundaries on all sides. Kosmas, a medieval monk and historian, wrote in 1125, "It is almost as if it were one continuous mountain range encircling and protecting this country." [1] Within this protective circle, majestic rivers flow among heavily farmed plateaus and rolling, wooded hillsides.

The deep love and reverence that Czechs have for the beauty of their country is reflected in their national anthem. While the anthems of other countries are usually rousing compositions with lyrics that boast about the nation's glorious past, the Czech national anthem, "Where Is My Homeland?" celebrates the forests, mountains, and rivers of the Republic's stunning landscape.

MOUNTAIN BORDERS

The Czech Republic's borders are formed by six major mountain ranges. The rugged Český Les and Sumava ranges form the Czech-German border in the southwest. Both are covered with thick woodlands and are subjected to harsh winter climates. The Krusne, or Ore Mountains, form the Czech Republic's northwestern boundary with Germany. This range includes a unique formation of head-shaped and conical hills (the Ceske stredohori), which are remnants of volcanic activity millions of years ago. The range also includes a rugged sandstone ridge rich in zinc and copper.

The country's highest mountains are piled across the Czech Republic's northern edge, along its northern border with Poland. The Krkonoše, or Giant Mountains, are rounded from age and cut by wide shallow valleys covered in spruce forests. Similar to the famous Swiss Alps in climate and breathtaking beauty, many of these stunning snowcapped peaks rise to higher than 5,000 feet. One of the more well known is Mount Sněžka, at 5,256 feet, which is visited by thousands of tourists every year.

Farther east along the Polish-Czech border lie the Jeseník Mountains. Also appreciated for its beauty, this range offers more than just mountain peaks, however. A glacial basin called Velka Kotlina, accessible only to experienced hikers, offers natural protection to an assortment of plant and animal life that includes unusual species of newts and lizards, as well as meadows covered with rare flowers and peat-bog plants. The Velka Kotlina is so isolated that some plant and animal species have remained untouched by changes that wiped out similar organisms elsewhere in Europe.

Southeast of the Jeseník Mountains, straddling almost the entire border that the Czech Republic shares with Slovakia, lie the towering Carpathian Mountains. Millions of years of water erosion have formed deep gorges and canyons along the western edge of the range.

MAJESTIC FORESTS

Although more than half the nation's land has been cleared for farming and industry, large areas of dense forests still cover

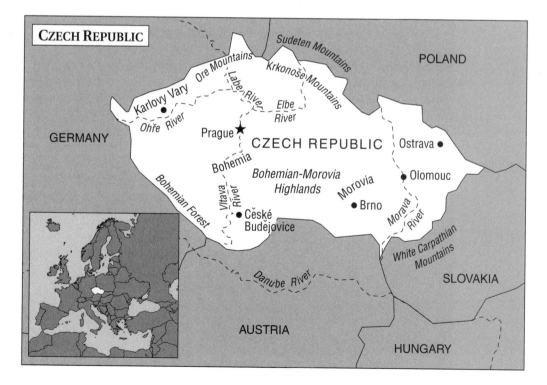

FEAR OF FLOODS

Some Czechs call the Flood of 1997 the worst in their history. It made international headlines when it killed forty-eight people, left more than four thousand homeless, and caused billions of dollars in damages. In three weeks, floodwaters devastated more than a third of Czech lands. It was even worse than the Great Flood of 1965.

The 1997 flood was indeed catastrophic, but probably not the worst in Czech history. Church records exist of severe floods dating back as far as the thirteenth century. The damage was particularly devastating in the years 1445, 1501, and 1721. Until the 1880s, it was up to individual local communities to control floodwaters by building dikes and canals. The Habsburg rulers of the Austro-Hungarian empire were the first to experience the annual flood threats on a more national level by building floodgates at points along the entire length of the Danube River and most of its tributaries, thereby regulating the flow of water.

Although mother nature cannot always be controlled, many Czechs are frustrated because they know much of the damage could have been prevented. After World War II, Western European countries such as Germany and Austria had to rebuild much of their bombed-out cities and countryside. In the process, they used modern technology to build hydraulic plants along the Rhine, Danube, and other rivers. The plants were built to provide a cheap source of electrical power, but they were also useful in controlling floodwaters. Czechoslovakia and other Eastern European countries under Soviet control needed cheap electrical power, but they did not have the funds or the technology to build hydroelectric projects until the 1970s. Even then, disputes over project design and material shortages delayed many of the projects another ten years. Some were never completed. One joint project between Czechoslovakia and Hungary was started in 1978 but was put on hold ten years later to battle a dispute in the World Court at The Hague, Netherlands, over the diversion of the water. A decision wasn't reached until early 2000.

The new Czech government has worked hard in its short existence to get energy and flood-control projects in place, but even hydroelectric plants and new dams and canal systems can divert only so much water.

more than one-third of the Czech Republic, mostly in these mountainous areas.

The Bohemian Forest, located along the southwest Sumava Mountain range, is a heavily wooded mountain region that stretches for about seventy-eight miles along the German and Austrian borders. Most of the vegetation consists of beech, spruce, and pine trees, some dating back more than four thousand years. For centuries these forests have supplied the needs of European builders and craftsmen, as well as fired the imaginations of some of Europe's finest writers and composers.

These thick forests have prevented the southwestern regions of the Czech Republic from becoming densely populated. The few towns that did spring up in this often harsh climate, such as České Budějovice, were built as mining towns because of the area's rich iron and gold ore deposits. The few hardy farmers who chose to settle here had to work hard to clear the dense forest so they would have enough fertile soil to produce crops like barley and hops used to brew beer.

Forests of coniferous (evergreen) trees cover large areas of the Ore Mountains in the northwest. Although the government converted a sizable part of the area's forests into national parks in 1963, it has not been able to protect the trees from extensive pollution damage. Estimates suggest that as many as 25 percent of the trees have been badly damaged by acid rain, due to massive industrialization and coal use in nearby cities.

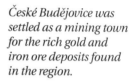

České Budějovice was settled as a mining town for the rich gold and iron ore deposits found in the region.

THE DANGERS OF ACID RAIN

Summer rains that once nourished Czech farmlands and turned its forests a lush green now spread deadly air and water pollution, which is taking a large toll on the environment throughout northern Czech lands.

The brown coal used in thermal power stations, as fuel in homes, and as raw material in the chemical industry is relatively cheap and plentiful, but it is not an acceptable trade-off for the terrible air pollution it causes. Levels of choking smog and sulfur pollutants are so high in cities such as Prague that on particularly cold days in winter, when large numbers of people are burning coal for heat, residents have to wear surgical masks when they go outside.

Since World War II, in an effort to decrease their dependence on fossil fuels, Czechs have built hydroelectric and nuclear power plants along the rivers, but these, too, pose increasing hazards. Pressure is building from concerned citizens, not just in the Czech Republic but from all over Europe, to shut down the nuclear plants to avoid potential accidents.

THE PROVINCES OF BOHEMIA AND MORAVIA

The lands that make up today's Czech Republic have been historically divided into two distinct provinces: Bohemia in the west and Moravia in the east. Although they both have rolling

Acid rain takes its toll on the evergreens that once flourished in the Ore Mountains.

farmland bordered by forests and protective mountain ranges, the regions have developed differently.

Bohemia, the larger of the two, has always been more densely populated and more prosperous than Moravia. The population and prosperity can be attributed to two factors: Bohemia's more central European location has provided its residents with opportunities to grow rich through trade, and most of Bohemia is on an elevated plateau of fertile farmland. The plateau is excellent for planting such diverse crops as wheat, rye, barley, oats, potatoes, and beets. Industrial areas also thrived on the Bohemian plateau because mineral resources such as silver, iron, mercury, lead, zinc, gold, tin, graphite, coal, and uranium were abundant in the surrounding foothills.

In neighboring Moravia, the rolling hills are not as fertile or easy to farm as the Bohemian plateau, so farmers are generally less prosperous than in Bohemia. Moravia also has fewer mineral resources and as a result, fewer industrial cities.

Spires rise above surrounding farmland in densely populated central Bohemia.

WATERWAYS

Bohemia and Moravia do share one important geographical feature: Because both provinces are landlocked, prior to the

The Vltava River begins in the Bohemian Forest and runs through the city of Prague.

twentieth century Czechs depended on their rivers to transport farm crops and ore to markets all over Europe. Today these rivers are not heavily used as trade routes and move only about 5 percent of the nation's cargo because it is cheaper and faster to move goods by truck or rail.

Rivers still play a large role in the Czech Republic, however. They generate electricity through the use of dams and hydroelectric plants, powering homes, factories, and businesses. Dams such as those built on the upper part of the Morava River have changed the Czech countryside by creating rugged canyons and large man-made lakes that have become popular recreation spots.

The Czech Republic has three major rivers: the Labe, the Morava, and the Vltava. The Labe River (also known as the Elbe River) starts in the Krkonoše (Giant) Mountains, then flows southward through the Bohemian basin before curving westward through the Ore Mountains into Germany, where it eventually flows into the North Sea.

The Morava River in the eastern part of the country flows from north to south through a valley in the Moravian lowlands. Moravia takes its name from the Morava River, which divides the province almost in two. Although some industrial centers and mining towns have sprung up in the river valley, Moravia remains mostly an agricultural region. The Morava and several smaller rivers eventually flow south and empty into the Danube River, one of Europe's busiest and longest waterways.

The country's third river is the Vltava, which is also known as the Moldau River. The Vltava River starts in the Bohemian Forest in the south, then flows northward through Prague—before emptying into the Labe (or Elbe) River. For fifteen centuries historic battles have been fought in Bohemia to control this river and its bridges. Whoever controlled the river, controlled the politically and economically important city of Prague.

Czech waters have become legendary for their alleged healing powers. Hundreds of thousands of people, including many of Europe's wealthy and famous, have flocked to western Bohemia since the days of the Middle Ages to soak their bodies in the mineral-rich waters of its mountain spas. Many people believe that these waters can cure everything from respiratory tract and urological disorders to heart disease and digestive problems.

The Czech Republic capitalizes on this belief and exports its famous mineral water. Western Bohemia has been bottling its local mineral water in earthen bottles with tin caps and exporting it all over Europe since the late nineteenth century.

CLIMATE

The Czech Republic's climate is as dramatic as its rugged, beautiful geography. The damp continental climate of central Europe, which covers most of the Czech Republic, is responsible for generally warm, showery summers and cold, snowy winters. But temperature and precipitation levels can fluctuate

MY BEAUTIFUL HOMELAND

The romantic and historical landscapes of Bohemia and Moravia have inspired writers, painters, and composers for years. A dedication to their beauty is the long musical poem *Ma Vlast* or *Where Is My Homeland*, written by the Czech composer Bedřich Smetana in the late 1870s. This music describes the Vltava (also known as the Moldau) River's dramatic flow over rocky riverbeds during a spring thunderstorm. It is still a favorite concert piece of symphonies throughout the world. Today it is also the new Czech Republic's national anthem.

Kde domov muj?	Where is my homeland?
Kde domov muj, kde domov muj?	Where is my homeland, where is my homeland?
Voda huci po lucinach,	Waters murmur through the meadows,
bory sumi po skalinach,	forests rustle all over the rocky hills,
v sade skvi se jara kvet,	spring blossoms glitter in the orchards,
zemsky raj to na pohled!	paradise on earth to look at!
A to je ta krasna zeme,	This is a beautiful country,
zeme ceska domov muj,	the Czech country, my homeland,
zeme ceska domov muj!	the Czech country, my homeland!

considerably within these seasons and cause unpredictable weather changes. July is the hottest month everywhere in the country; January is the coldest. From December through February, temperatures push below freezing even in the lowlands and are often bitter cold in the mountains.

Although less precipitation falls in winter than in summer, the Czech Republic has no real dry season. Even the long, sunny hot spells of summer tend to be broken by sudden, heavy thunderstorms. In the spring, sudden climate changes can and often do bring disaster in the form of floods. A rise in temperature causes mountain snow to melt, swelling the rivers that come crashing down the hillsides to wreak havoc on towns and cities in the valleys.

TOWNS AND CITIES

For most of their history, Czech people depended on the rich resources of their lands to make a living. Although in the mid–twentieth century, before the end of World War II, the country was largely agricultural, today fewer than 20 percent of Czechs are involved in farming. The rest work in urban areas.

The large state-run farming collectives that were formed under the Communist regime in the early 1950s were divided up and privatized in the 1990s. After the collapse of the Soviet Union, the government still provided farmers with subsidies and with scientific and ecological advice. Crops include wheat, barley, sugar beets, cabbage, corn, rye, oats, and potatoes. One of the biggest export crops is hops, which is exported to major breweries throughout the world. Farmers throughout the Czech Republic also raise livestock, including cows and pigs.

Today, 30 percent of the population still lives in small, rural towns, each consisting of fewer than five thousand people. Approximately fifteen thousand of these towns exist. The remaining 70 percent of the Czech population lives in urban, industrial areas, primarily in northern Bohemia.

The largest city, Prague, is also the nation's capital. Prague has been at the heart of Czech history since the Great Bohemian

The Czech Republic's capital of Prague is said to have been founded by a Bohemian warrior-princess named Libussa.

empire was established over a thousand years ago. (According to legend, Prague was founded by a Bohemian warrior-princess named Libussa during the eighth century. The women of Bohemia were apparently so inspired by her that when she died, they rose up and stormed the land in protest of male domination.)

The "City of 100 Spires," as Prague is often called, lies on the Vltava River in the geographical center of Bohemia. A beautiful old city of ancient castles, bridges, and cathedrals, Prague attracts tourists from all over the world who come to view its varied stunning architecture. The historic Old Town section of Prague was originally built in the ninth century on the shores of the winding Vltava River, down a mountainside from a huge

The town of Karlovy Vary contains hot springs believed to have healing powers.

BOHEMIA'S ENCHANTED FORESTS

The Bohemian Forest, Český Les, extends roughly 150 miles along the mountainous Czech-German border and into Austria. In addition to its primeval stands of thick, overgrown trees, there are sublime marshes, swamps, caves, and peat bogs. Many of the crumbling stone castles atop the rock formations jutting out from towering mountainsides look as menacing and formidable as they must have looked in medieval days. It's no wonder that so many European fairy tales are set in this forest, or that so many composers and writers have found inspiration in its eerie myths and legends. Famed Czech composer Antonín Dvořák wrote an entire opera, *The Water Goblin,* based on a slimy green-haired demon who, it is said, still haunts the forest's lakes.

stone castle. Over the centuries Prague was invaded by numerous foreign armies, including the Swedes, Hungarians, Austrians, Germans, and Soviets. Many of the old inner city buildings that were covered over with plaster fronts under the Communist regime have now been restored to their old magnificence. Today the historical district surrounding the Old Town Square is home to some of the most exclusive and fashionable shops in Europe. It is also the center of an expanding artistic community of art galleries and museums and a thriving music scene featuring everything from classical symphonies to rap music to jazz.

Brno, with a population of 400,000, is only half as large as Prague, but has an equally vibrant history as a center of art and trade. Founded as the capital of Moravia in the fourteenth century, it became a thriving textile center during the Austro-Hungarian empire. Today Brno is known for its Catholic monastery, its university, and its many annual trade fairs, as well as for a well-attended annual motorcycle grand prix.

Another important Czech city in the heart of Moravia is Olomouc, a youthful, laid-back university center on the Morava River. Local legends claim that it was first founded by Julius Caesar. Like Brno, Olomouc served as the Moravian capital for several centuries—until it was occupied and looted by Swedish troops from 1642 to 1650. Tourists flock to the city for its historical architecture.

Karlovy Vary (also known as Carlsbad) is a famous Bohemian spa town founded (according to legend) by King Charles IV after he and his dog were scalded by a hot spring while hunting in the Slavkov Forest. Believing that the mineral waters there possess healing properties, people have visited the town over the centuries, including writers such as Johann Goethe and composers such as Ludwig von Beethoven, Johann Sebastian Bach, and Richard Wagner.

The Czech Republic's larger cities face the same problems most large cities face today: crime, traffic congestion, a growing homeless population, urban decay, and pollution. Many city inhabitants are choosing to buy and restore old houses in surrounding rural areas, so suburbs are growing and the inner cities are deteriorating. The Czech government is promoting the restoration of old buildings to save the architecture and offering subsidies to the cities' artists, writers, and musicians to strengthen the cultural scene.

LOVE OF COUNTRY

Czechs have fought hard for their existing independence and cultural identity. Whether farmers or city dwellers, Bohemians or Moravians, older people who remember grim Communist rule or younger people growing up in freedom and democracy,

HURRY! BOOK NOW!

Many travel agencies offer specialized tours of the Czech Republic. Some advertise spectacular train and bus tours of the scenic Czech countryside, while others focus on the rich culture and history of its capital city, Prague. There are architectural tours, even tours that sample regional cuisines. Lately, though, some of the popular (and often most expensive) tours take bird-watchers from all over the world on hiking trips through the Czech Republic's seven federal wildlife preserves—to catch glimpses of rare birds. During the day, hikers load themselves down with binoculars and camera equipment and trudge over miles of mountain trails and marshy peat bogs in search of such rare species as bluethroats, crakes, purple herons, black storks, white-tailed eagles, pygmy owls, and red-crested tits. In the evenings, tour guests can enjoy private outdoor concerts listening to classical, gothic, and Bohemian folk music in castle courtyards.

throughout history, one thing has always united them: their deeply rooted love of country. Czechs are not the only ones who value their Bohemian and Moravian homelands. For centuries its rich resources and location in the heart of Europe has made the Bohemian-Moravian area a political football among its often tyrannical neighbors.

2

EARLY HISTORY

The struggle for control of Czech homelands is a long and vivid one. Czech history dates back at least twenty-five centuries. The first known settlers of what is today the Czech Republic, a Celtic people called the Boii, arrived in the fourth century B.C. The Latin name for Bohemia, "Boiohaemum," is derived from their name. Over the next few centuries Germanic tribes chased out the Czech Celts from the east. Starting in the third century A.D., waves of Slavic peoples began migrating west from Russia, not just into Czech lands, but into Poland, Hungary, and Yugoslavia as well. By the seventh century A.D., the Germanic tribes had abandoned the area to the Slavs.

FORMATION OF THE GREAT MORAVIAN EMPIRE

The Czech Slavs settled into many small, independent villages without any kind of unifying political leader. They called themselves Moravians, after the Morava River along which many of them settled. They would have been chased out of the area by the Avars, a powerful Asian tribe living on the plains of Hungary, if a Moravian leader named Samo had not convinced them that the only way to protect their lands was to unite.

Even united, however, the Moravian Slavs were not strong enough to fight the Avars by themselves. Samo asked for help from Charlemagne, a powerful ruler of the Franks, a Germanic people to the west. Charlemagne had already united much of western and central Europe and helped convert it to Christianity. With Charlemagne's help, the Moravian Slavs defeated the Avars.

By the early ninth century, the area had grown into a flourishing empire, which included Moravia, Bohemia, southern parts of present-day Poland and Silesia, and the western part of Hungary. The Great Moravian empire became a prosperous crossroads of trade and new ideas. It was during this period that the Moravians accepted Christianity and developed their own alphabet, two significant developments.

Although the Moravians were exposed to Christianity when they enlisted the Franks to help them in their war against the Avars, few converted to the new religion for two reasons: None of them understood Latin, the language in which Roman Catholicism was being preached in parts of western Europe, and they didn't have a written language into which the Christian Bible could be translated. An offshoot of Roman Catholicism called Byzantine Christianity started developing farther east, in Constantinople. When the Moravian king heard about it, he requested that the Byzantine Church send representatives to his court. The two men who came, Cyril and Methodius, spoke fluent Slavic and quickly converted the king. To help spread the new religion to his people, the king asked Cyril and Methodius to create a new alphabet for the spoken Slavic language. This Cyrillic alphabet (named after Cyril) is still in use in much of Eastern Europe today.

Charlemagne joined forces with the Moravian Slavs to defeat the Avars.

In 903, the Great Moravian empire was again threatened, this time by invading Hungarians; the invaders were successful. The national government, which had unified the people and given them a prosperous trading economy, collapsed. The Moravians reverted back to a society of small, isolated villages. They lived that way for the better part of a century.

PŘEMYSLID DYNASTY

Up until the tenth century, the eastern Czech lands of Moravia were more settled and unified than the Bohemian region to the west. In the tenth century the Přemyslids of Bohemia changed all that. They built a powerful dynasty by systematically murdering the entire

Cyril and Methodius visit the Moravian king and convert him to Byzantine Christianity.

families of anyone who threatened their right to the Bohemian throne. Some of the Přemyslids were so vicious in their competition for power that they killed each other. For example, Wenceslas I (the Good King Wenceslas mentioned in the Christmas carol) was made a saint soon after his brother, King Boleslav the Cruel, murdered him in 929.

In spite of the family's bloody rise to power, the Přemyslids made some notable accomplishments. They did much to increase the power and prestige of the Czech peoples. They quickly took over the helpless Moravia, then set about conquering other neighboring lands such as Silesia and Slovakia to expand their empire. During the 1100s and 1200s, Bohemia flourished as a crossroads for several major continental trade routes. Increased trade led to the development of cities and large towns. In spite of their sometimes barbaric political acts, the Přemyslids had a strong interest in the exchange of cultural ideas, especially with the Holy Roman Empire.

THE CZECH MIDDLE AGES

By the time Prague was founded in 1234, Bohemia was considered one of Europe's more economically and culturally advanced states. This was the Middle Ages, however, when most of Europe (including Bohemia) was still a feudal society. The land was owned by a handful of aristocrats and farmed by peasant serfs who were really no better off than slaves. But in cities like Prague, society was becoming more complex.

In addition to aristocrats and serfs, medieval Bohemian society had burghers (shop owners and traders). Unlike serfs, burghers could earn money and improve their standard of living. Successful burghers bought houses, furniture, clothing, and other possessions. They drank at taverns, gave donations to the church, and even went to concerts and plays. This not only stimulated the economy by making work for other burghers, but it also invigorated culture by giving artists a chance to earn a living.

Besides the burghers, medieval Bohemia had another important group of citizens: German settlers. To help increase the empire's population and further stimulate the economy, the Přemyslids invited Germans to colonize the previously uninhabited regions of Bohemia and Moravia that bordered on German lands. Although the German shop owners, traders, and peasants who settled there learned to speak Czech and became part of the local community, they also kept their native language and many of their cultural traditions.

At the beginning of the thirteenth century, the Czech kingdom was flourishing. The more rich and powerful the Přemyslids became, however, the more they wanted. The Přemyslid king Otakar II was so wealthy and powerful that after he defeated the armies of neighboring Hungary in 1256 and 1260 and then took over the Alpine Mountain region that is known today as Austria and southern Germany, he became known as the "King of Gold and Iron." His new status didn't last long, however.

Otakar II was so busy expanding his empire that he didn't pay much attention when a German named Rudolf Habsburg was elected ruler of the Holy Roman Empire. In 1278, when Otakar's troops were off fighting the Hungarians again, Rudolf marched in and reclaimed the Alpine region with the help of several German princes. Rudolf's Holy Roman Empire was expanding rapidly, too. He immediately made Austria its seat of power.

That same year, Otakar died fighting the Hungarians and was succeeded to the Bohemian throne by his son, Wenceslas II (1278–1305). The economy flourished under his reign. Trade with neighboring countries increased and peace was made

Under King Wenceslas II (center), Bohemia enjoyed prosperity and peaceful coexistence with its neighbor, Hungary.

with former rival Hungary. When he died in 1305, his young son Wenceslas III took the throne. Wenceslas III was the last male member of the Přemyslids line, and his untimely death a year later ended the four-hundred-year Přemyslid dynasty.

THE LUXEMBOURG DYNASTY AND KING CHARLES IV

The throne next went to an aristocrat named John of Luxembourg, who married Wenceslas III's eighteen-year-old sister to gain the support of the Czech nobility. John was fourteen when he ascended the throne, but even when he grew up, he was not a very effective ruler. He was more interested in dressing up in armor and leading his men in battle than he was in running his empire. In 1346, he died fighting on the side of his distant French relative, Charles.

Charles IV promoted cultural and economic growth.

John's successor, his son Wenceslas IV (who became known as Charles IV), turned out to be much more interested in ruling, and much more capable. Charles IV was well educated. He spoke five languages fluently and quickly proved to be a skillful diplomat. He also had made some influential friends during his school days in Paris, including Pope Clement VI.

Charles IV was a dilettante (a lover of the arts) and did much to promote culture and economic growth, especially in the capital city, Prague. He not only supported artists and musicians, but he also ordered the building of monumental bridges, castles, and cathedrals. He founded Charles University, the first center of higher education in central Europe, and promoted the Czech beer and wine industries. Prague became the official seat of the Holy Roman Empire, and Charles IV took the title of Holy Roman Emperor. Because of many cultural and humanitarian achievements of his reign, Charles IV is often called the Father of the Czech Nation.

But as much as Charles IV was revered, his oldest son and successor, Wenceslas IV, was despised. (His name is confusing because his father, Charles, was also born with the name Wenceslas IV.) Wenceslas IV, who ruled from 1378 to 1419, was especially unpopular with the burgher class. He was not a supporter of the

Commissioned by Charles IV, the Charles Bridge still stands as a monument to Czech cultural achievement.

arts, nor did he commission public building projects to employ the poor, as his father had. Instead of promoting trade and business, he angered shopkeepers and traders by frequently (and often unfairly) accusing them of cheating their customers. His favorite punishment was to have them thrown to their deaths off the Charles Bridge. Wenceslas IV was known to be fond of drinking, and was even more brutal and arbitrary than usual when he was intoxicated.

JAN HUS AND THE HUSSITES

Wenceslas IV infuriated Czech merchants and traders, and so did the Catholic Church that the king and other nobles supported. A large part of the taxes that burghers paid ended up in the pockets of church leaders, who became wealthy and powerful landowners. The burghers were not allowed the same religious privileges that Czech aristocrats enjoyed. Under church law, only aristocrats could take communion (consecrated bread) and buy their way out of mortal sin. That meant that aristocrats would not have to go to hell when they died, or serve any kind of penance in this life, even for the sin of murder, providing that they paid the church enough money.

So when a preacher named Jan Hus started traveling through-out the country publicly criticizing the Catholic Church for its corrupt materialism and unfair elitism, he got the burghers' attention. Hus had other radical ideas about the Catholic Church that appealed to Czech peasants. Against church law, he conducted his sermons in Czech instead of in Latin so that the illiterate peasants could participate. Hus's ideas were extremely dangerous during a time when people even suspected of questioning church doctrine were sentenced to death by torture. When word of Hus's preachings reached the pope in 1415, he was outraged and ordered Hus burned at the stake for heresy. Instead of squashing Hus's radical ideas, however, the pope's action only angered and united Hus's supporters even more.

By 1419, the Hussites, as they called themselves, were so upset with the government in Prague for its support of the Catholic

JAN HUS VINDICATED AT LAST BY THE POPE

Czechs still consider the execution of Jan Hus almost six hundred years ago a terrible injustice. They consider it equally unjust that outside of his native Czech lands, this great religious reformer has been almost forgotten. In 1999 the head of the Catholic Church, Pope John Paul II, took steps to right both of those injustices. Because he was born in Poland, the pope took special interest in the peoples of eastern Europe. He wanted them to live in harmony with each other by learning to respect and understand each other's heritage. To help do that, he formed a number of symposiums made up of Catholic and Protestant scholars, one of which was commissioned to study and possibly reevaluate the Catholic Church's official position on Jan Hus.

The symposium concluded that Hus was not a heretic but a moral and religious man who had the interests of the Czech people at heart and did not deserve to die. In December 1999, in a speech given to a group of visiting Czechs, including President Václav Havel, the pope expressed his deep regret for the cruel death inflicted on Jan Hus in 1415. He commended Hus's "moral courage in the face of adversity and death" and promised that the Catholic Church would continue to study and discuss his writings. Czechs hope that Hus will now take his rightful place in history and be honored as a passionate reformer with sound ideas and fierce integrity.

ŽIŽKA, THE ONE-EYED MILITARY GENIUS

Little is known of Jan Žižka's early life except that he grew up at the court of King Wenceslas IV of Bohemia. In his late teens he became a mercenary (a paid soldier) and spent the next twenty years fighting for the neighboring Poles. When he finally returned to Bohemia in his late thirties, he learned about a Czech religious reformer named Jan Hus.

A memorial to Žižka, stands in Prague, Czech Republic.

Žižka immediately became one of Hus's most fervent followers. When Wenceslas died in 1419 and his anti-Hussite half-brother Sigismund attempted to ascend the Bohemian throne, Žižka organized a peasant resistance and made himself its military leader.

He was brilliant. In fact, Žižka was ahead of his time regarding military strategy. Up until that time, the cannons used in battle were so heavy they could be used only to defend the buildings they were mounted on or near. Žižka devised a way to take his cannon with him by having it mounted on specially modified farm wagons. Although the wagons were cumbersome, the cannon still gave him tactical advantage over his less well armed enemies. He was also an expert at other tactical strategies, such as attacking with both infantry and cavalry at the same time, under a single command.

Žižka's passion and military genius made him practically unbeatable. He crushed Sigismund near Prague in 1420, in spite of losing an eye in battle. He continued to lead his forces to victory against the Catholic Crusades, finally dying of plague in 1424. His Hussite armies were so inspired that they continued the fight without him for almost another fifteen years until finally facing defeat.

Strangely, although Žižka's tactical successes were well documented, it was another two hundred years before any other European military commanders adopted his methods. Swedish king Gustavus II Adolph became the first to reintroduce mobile artillery into battle in the seventeenth century. The weapons tactic became a European standard of battle.

Church that they stormed the Czech town hall and threw seven council members out a window to their deaths. Today this event is known as the First Defenestration of Prague. King Wenceslas IV was so upset when he heard about the deadly protest that he died of a heart attack. Wenceslas's brother, King Sigismund of Luxembourg, was supposed to succeed him, but was never able to take power. He spent the rest of his life fighting the Hussites for control of the throne. Even the five waves of crusaders the pope sent to help him couldn't defeat the determined Hussites.

Peace negotiations between the Hussites and opposing Catholic forces finally began in 1431 when a new pope came to power. In the Council of Basel, the Roman Catholic Church agreed to make communion available to everyone in Bohemia, regardless of their social status. The church also agreed to give up ownership of land and to create an independent Bohemian Catholic Church.

During the rest of the fifteenth century the Hussite movement spread and started gaining popularity even among Czech aristocrats. The Bohemian throne remained empty until Sigismund

A fifteenth-century drawing shows preacher Jan Hus burning at the stake for his alleged heresy against the Catholic Church.

JOSEPH II: THE ENLIGHTENED DESPOT

Joseph II was probably the only popular Habsburg in the Czech lands. He still appears in numerous Czech folk legends, poems, and songs. For a long time after his rule, "Joseph" was the most common first name in Bohemia. He died in 1790 at the age of forty-nine. During his lifetime Joseph II enacted more than six thousand reforms that, for the first time, recognized the rights of common people and improved their standard of living. Joseph still retained the totalitarian power of a monarch, but he was considered enlightened.

Joseph learned about the desperate poverty of the people in his empire by traveling extensively in disguise. He saw how serfs lived their lives as virtual slaves. Workers born on the land of a lord—and their families—were still considered the lord's property. Not only could the lord force surfs to work grueling hours, he could also choose not to pay them and could punish them however and whenever he wanted. Serfs were not allowed to move from place to place, to get married, or even to learn to read without the permission of the lord on whose manor they lived.

One of Joseph's first edicts was to make these serfs free men. Legally, a lord could no longer stop his employees or their families from moving, refuse to pay them, or physically abuse them. That new freedom of movement allowed people to move to urban areas which would soon be booming with industrial jobs. Not surprisingly, the edict was immensely unpopular with the Czech aristocracy.

Another of Joseph's edicts also proved unpopular with some people. Until Joseph gained the throne, the Habsburg empire forced Catholicism on people throughout its domain. Some Hussites either converted or fled the country, but most simply pretended to be Catholics. Joseph opposed the idea of forcing spiritual beliefs on anyone else. He believed that everyone, rich or poor, had the right to choose his or her own religion. He therefore granted civil rights to Protestants, Lutherans, Calvinists, Greek Orthodox Christians, and Jews.

The third of Joseph's most important reform edicts was the abolition of censorship. This extraordinary and unprecedented act gave people the right and freedom to openly criticize even the Habsburg throne. Joseph was enlightened enough to realize that the only way to know if he was ruling effectively—if his reforms were doing any good—was to make himself open to public criticism.

finally admitted defeat and gave up all claims to it. After Sigismund no one could claim a hereditary right to the throne, so Czech nobles chose George of Podebrady, a Hussite aristocrat, to take power. George, who became known as the Hussite King, quickly gained a reputation throughout Europe for being a skillful diplomat and someone who wanted European nations to live in peace. Unfortunately, no one else in Europe seemed to want peace, especially Catholic rulers like Hungary's King Matthias Corvinus, who did not like the idea of a Hussite on the Czech throne. Corvinus declared war against George of Podebrady. The war lasted until George died and was succeeded by Vladislav Jagellon, a Catholic noble.

Meanwhile, the Austrian (and Catholic) Habsburgs had gained control of a large part of western Europe. They felt that Czech lands would make an impressive addition to their empire, so

Ferdinand I claimed the Czech throne for the Habsburg dynasty.

when King Jagellon died in 1526, Ferdinand I of Habsburg immediately stepped in to claim the Czech throne. He justified the takeover by stating that he was the late King Jagellon's brother-in-law. The royal Habsburg family, already a powerful dynasty in Europe, continued to rule Czech lands until the early twentieth century.

3

FIRST STIRRINGS OF NATIONALISM

The Habsburg empire was strong and prosperous and Czech lands flourished under its rule, both culturally and economically. But that didn't mean that Czechs adopted the Germanic culture of their rulers. On the contrary, over the years, Czechs became increasingly aware of their unique cultural heritage, and their resentment of Habsburg control over their national identity grew.

THE HABSBURG DYNASTY

Habsburg king Ferdinand was unpopular with Czechs right from the start, especially among Czech nobility. Not only did he limit their wealth and political power, but he also tried to increase the political and economic power the Catholic Church had over Czech lands. By this time, a majority of Czech aristocrats had become Hussites. Even though the Czech economy was prospering, the nobles were becoming increasingly dissatisfied with Habsburg rule.

Ferdinand was succeeded by Maximilian II, who was succeeded by Rudolf II. The cultural Renaissance, which was sweeping through Europe, had reached its peak in Prague. The city had become a progressive center of European art, science, and education. Rudolf II (1576–1611) loved the city; when he ascended the Austrian throne, he officially moved the Habsburg court from Vienna to Prague.

Rudolf II moved the Habsburg court from Vienna to Prague.

Rudolf II collected great art—including works by Leonardo da Vinci, Michelangelo, and Raphael—and he supported scientists such as Tycho Brahe, Johannes Kepler, and Copernicus. In spite of Rudolf's love and support of Czech culture, however, he was a Catholic Habsburg and the Czech nobility still hated him.

Government officials are thrown from a window during a rebellion at Prague Castle.

When he was forced by his family to resign because he suffered bouts of dementia, the nobility saw the perfect opportunity to rise up against the Habsburgs and get rid of them for good. They started their revolt in 1618 with what was becoming a Czech tradition: defenestration. This time various government officials were thrown out of a tower window at Prague Castle. It became known as the Second Defenestration of Prague.

Although the rebellion of the Czech nobility had the widespread support of the Czech people, it didn't last long. After the Czechs were badly defeated by Habsburg troops in the Battle of the White Mountain in 1620, the Habsburgs made sure no one else would soon get the same rebellious ideas. They immediately executed twenty-seven of the nobles in Prague's Old Town Square, then hung their decapitated heads from towers and

The standard of living improved for the Czech people under the leadership of Maria Theresa.

lampposts all over town as a grisly reminder. No one was allowed to take them down for a year.

The Habsburgs didn't stop there. They banned all religions other than Catholicism and forced all Hussite Czechs to convert. The property of Hussite nobles was confiscated and given to loyal Catholics. Many Czech Hussites fled the country. Only a very few of those who stayed had the courage to continue to secretly practice their religion. Because so many Czechs were killed in the uprising, fewer people were left to pay taxes, so taxes were raised. Trade declined, businesses failed, and the Czech economy went into a depression.

Not until a century later, when the Habsburg rulers Maria Theresa and her son, Joseph II, came to the throne, did Czech living conditions finally improve again. During their reigns in the eighteenth and early nineteenth centuries, the Industrial Revolution had swept Europe and was creating a demand for coal and other Czech natural resources. It was a logical choice to build the Austrian empire's first factories on Czech mountainsides because they were close to mining areas and they could harness the waterpower of streams and rivers. The Habsburgs built railway lines connecting Czech mining and industrial towns with the rest of Europe to move manufactured goods, which had a tremendous effect in revitalizing Czech trade.

Industrialization brought prosperity to Czech lands and with prosperity came a renewed interest in promoting the arts. Scientific research and technological inventions were strongly encouraged and social issues such as religious tolerance and public education became increasingly important.

CZECH NATIONAL REVIVAL MOVEMENT

Czechs in the nineteenth century were proud of their economic prosperity. But their pride went deeper than that. Artists and writers stirred up pride in the history, language, and rich cultural traditions. The Austrian Habsburgs with their Germanic background and language ruled the Czechs, but they viewed themselves as neither Austrian nor German. As the Czechs' appreciation of their cultural identity deepened, so did their resentment of foreign rule. Like the Slovaks, the Hungarians, and most other nationalities under Habsburg rule, Czechs wanted the right to govern themselves. This movement in culture and politics became known as the Czech National Revival Movement.

The members of the revival movement were divided. Half wanted more control of their own government while still remaining under the protection and stability of the Austro-Hungarian empire. The more radical half wanted complete, democratic self-rule and total independence from the Habsburg monarchy. Rumors of revolution spread among radical political leaders and university students, not just in Czech lands but throughout the Austro-Hungarian empire. By the middle of the nineteenth century, political tensions had continued to increase, but the Habsburgs kept the rebellions under control.

By the 1860s, however, the Habsburgs decided that if they did not make some concessions to their increasingly discontented subjects, they risked open revolution. Their solution was to transform the absolute Austro-Hungarian monarchy into a "constitutional monarchy." As far as the Czechs were concerned, that made little difference. The Habsburgs still ruled a good part of Europe with an iron fist even if their powers were technically limited by a constitution. If anything, this action served only to unite the different factions of the Czech revival movement. After that, almost everyone felt that Czechs would have any say in governing themselves only when they were completely independent.

The Czechs may have agreed that independence was what they wanted, but they were still split into conflicting political parties. Some wanted an independent Czech state that kept at least some economic and political ties to the Austro-Hungarian federation, while others wanted total, unqualified independence. Neither party was sure how to go about achieving its goal. Although political divisions grew deeper as the nineteenth century drew to a close, culturally, the Czech National Revival Movement reached a pinnacle. The Czech language, which had almost completely fallen into disuse, was rediscovered. Novelists and

THE SOKOLS

For many people, the Czech National Revival Movement meant more than the Czech people connecting with their cultural heritage and political strengths; it meant taking pride in their physical strength as well. The Sokols were a gymnastic society with a strong philosophy of Czech nationalism. Named after the Czech word for *falcon*, the organization was founded in 1862 by two friends—

The Sokols at practice.

Jindrich Fugner and Miroslav Tyrs. They modeled it after a German gymnastic organization called Turnvereine, which had played a strong role in promoting German nationalism in the 1840s. They also based it on Darwin's recently published theory of the survival of the fittest. The Sokols wanted to prepare for what could be a long and difficult struggle to gain independence by making sure they were in the best physical condition. The group believed that Czech nationalism could be achieved only through a combination of physical and spiritual training and a thorough education in the arts and sciences. Neighborhood Sokol clubs, where people of all ages practiced gymnastics, opened all over the country. Often huge rallies were held in larger Czech cities in which clubs gathered to rehearse and perform complex physical drills.

By the beginning of World War I, more than fifteen thousand men and women had joined the Sokols. The organization played a major role in unifying the nation of Czechoslovakia that was created when the war ended in 1918. The Nazis clearly understood the political and social power the movement had in Czechoslovakia and banned it when they invaded the country in 1939, eventually killing twenty-one thousand of its members.

Although people were forbidden to participate in Sokol gymnastics throughout the Nazi occupation of World War II, some members met secretly and kept enthusiasm for the movement alive. Membership soared again when the Nazis were defeated. The Communists who were in the process of taking total political control of Czechoslovakia, like the Nazis before them, understood the potential power the Sokol movement had in promoting Czech nationalism and independence. Instead of banning the movement, however, the Communists allowed its continued existence. They simply made it illegal for Sokol participants to hold any kind of mass rallies or other political gatherings of any kind.

But the Sokols survived even the Communists. The political focus of the movement was officially revived after the 1989 Velvet Revolution. Today's Sokol rallies draw large crowds of both young and old. Czechs who fled their native country in the twentieth century and settled in the United States and Great Britain took their Sokol enthusiasm with them. Sokol clubs can now be found in many Western nations.

historians wrote about Czech cultural traditions, folk myths, legends, and great Czech heroes. During the late nineteenth and early twentieth centuries, Czechs continued to gain worldwide recognition for outstanding achievements in art, literature, music, medicine, and science.

Czechs were not the only nationality under Austro-Hungarian rule who were becoming increasingly agitated about independence. These pressures increased over the next fifteen to twenty years until tensions in Europe finally exploded into war. On June 28, 1914, a radical Serbian nationalist named Gavrilo Princip assassinated the Archduke Francis Ferdinand, the heir to the Austrian throne. This event triggered the beginning of World War I. At the end of the conflict four years later, Czechs would finally be able to realize their dream of independence. But the dream would be short-lived and would be replaced by a nightmare.

The Archduke Francis Ferdinand (glancing at camera) was heir to the Austro-Hungarian throne when he was assassinated by a radical Serb.

WORLD WAR I AND CZECH INDEPENDENCE

World War I, also called the Great War, escalated into an international conflict which involved not only most of the nations of Europe, but also Russia, the United States, and parts of the Middle East and Asia. The war pitted the Central Powers, which included Germany, Austria-Hungary, and Turkey, against the Allies, which included France, Great Britain, Russia, Italy, Japan, and beginning in 1917, the United States. It took four years, but the Central Powers were defeated.

When World War I started in 1914, the Austro-Hungarian empire (which included the Czech lands of Bohemia and Moravia, and neighbors Serbia and Slovakia) immediately sided with Germany. Czech troops were drafted by the empire but they reluctantly fought. Most Czechs wanted peace, not a bloody, costly war. Also, they knew that an alliance between Germany and Austria would only strengthen the Austrian monarchy and lessen their prospects for independence. People living in Serbia, Slovakia, and Hungary, among others, also resented being under Austrian control and reluctantly fought as Austrian troops.

The anger and resentment over the war pulled the splintered Czech independence movement together. Many of its leaders (as well as those from neighboring Slovakia) had escaped to the United States, Britain, and other foreign countries when World War I broke out. They began working together to organize the movement and to gain international support for Czech and Slovakian independence. One of the movement's influential leaders was Tomáš Garrigue Masaryk, a former Czech university professor who fled to the United States in 1914. Masaryk worked closely with two other political leaders who had sought exile in the United States: a Czech lawyer named Edvard Benes and a Slovak astronomer named Milan Rastislav Stefanik.

Together the three men founded the Czech National Council in 1916, which the Allies officially recognized as the government-in-exile of an independent Czech-Slovak nation. The council contacted Czech and Slovak immigrants living in the United States and Britain and urged them to join the Allied fight against Germany on the Italian, French, and Russian fronts. So many responded that they formed their own military battalions. Their bravery helped give the Czech-Slovak independence movement worldwide recognition.

It was much riskier to organize the movement within the Czech lands. Freedom of speech did not exist. Newspapers were

completely censored, public meetings were outlawed, and any-one even suspected of disloyalty to the Austrian empire was arrested for treason and either executed or thrown in jail. Whatever organized resistance there was operated in small groups in a secret underground network. In 1917 Masaryk's spies advised him that there was growing evidence that the Central Powers were losing the war. Czech resistance groups became more open in their activities: They organized labor strikes and held massive, often violent demonstrations, in spite of Austrian retribution.

Czechs were reluctantly drawn into World War I on the side of the Central Powers.

In late 1917 the United States joined the Allies. President Woodrow Wilson listed the reasons for joining the war in a speech he called his "Fourteen Points." One of those points was important to Czechs both at home and abroad: The United States wanted to ensure "the freest opportunity of the autonomous development"[2] of the peoples of Austria-Hungary.

With U.S. help the Allies soon won the war, but the autonomous development President Wilson mentioned in his

Tomáš Garrigue Masaryk became the first president of the Czech Republic in 1918.

speech occurred before the war even ended. In May 1918, leaders of the Czech resistance movement living in the United States signed the Pittsburgh Convention, which officially approved the formation of a joint Czech and Slovakian nation. On November 14, 1918, these representatives formed a temporary parliament, which named Tomáš Garrigue Masaryk as the first acting president of the new Czechoslovak Republic.

THE FIRST REPUBLIC

The Czechoslovak Republic (CSR) was made up of Bohemia, Moravia, Silesia, Slovakia, and Ruthenia (which had been part of Russia). It also included the mountainous border areas along southwestern Bohemia, which had been settled centuries earlier by German immigrants. That area came to be known as the "Sudetenland," and the 3 million German Czechs who lived there made up more than 23 percent of the Czechoslovak population.

Czechoslovakia thrived under its new democratic government. Industry and private enterprise flourished; the economy grew so strong that the new country became one of the ten richest nations in the world. People had money to spend on culture and Czech art. Music and literature blossomed. Czechs also had the freedom to express their religious and political ideas. Even the Communist Party (which had been established in 1921) was legally allowed to exist. But neither Czechoslovakia's democracy nor its prosperity would last for long.

ECONOMIC DEPRESSION AND THE RISE OF FASCISM

At the end of the 1920s and the beginning of the 1930s, Europe, the United States, and much of the rest of the world fell into a devastating economic depression that lasted more than a decade. More than 1 million Czechs, including many who lived in the Sudetenland, lost their jobs. The German Czechs in the border areas began listening to an upcoming German leader named Adolf Hitler, who promised an end to their economic despair if the Sudetenland seceded from Czechoslovakia to become part of Germany. Hitler, of course, wanted that area so that he could expand German power and control. But his plans extended far beyond Sudetenland. He knew that causing divisions among the Czech people would weaken the country, thus allowing him to more easily gain control of all of Czechoslovakia.

The Czech government was already weakened by internal political turmoil. In 1935 President Masaryk became ill and resigned from office. He was succeeded by another influential leader of the Czech independence movement, Edvard Benes. But powerful as Benes had been helping form the new nation before and during World War I, he was a weak president. Political parties within Czechoslovakia had disintegrated into feuding splinter groups that couldn't agree on economic policies to steer the Czech economy out of its depression. The only party that became stronger and more organized was the Sudeten German Party. Eventually, it gained the support and control needed to run the government. Benes became nothing more than a figurehead, a puppet who did what the Sudeten German Party directed him to do.

The leader of this party was a former teacher named Konrad Henlein, who believed in the principles of the new National Socialist Party that Hitler had organized in the early 1930s. When Hitler rose to power, Henlein became his spokesperson in Czechoslovakia. Henlein worked hard to convince the Sudetenland Germans to secede from Czechoslovakia and join Germany. Even though such an action would cost Czechoslovakia a substantial portion of its population and geography and threaten its very independence as a nation, the major European powers—Britain, France, and Italy—were willing to comply if it meant Hitler would back off and leave the rest of Czechoslovakia (and the rest of Europe) alone. In September 1938 Germany, Great Britain, and France met in Munich to formalize the agreement.

The Munich Pact quickly proved disastrous. Czechoslovakia almost immediately lost about a third of its territory because as soon as Hitler took over the Sudetenland, Poland claimed the Těšín region to the north and Hungary annexed the southern parts of Slovakia and Ruthenia. Hitler, of course, had no intention of stopping with the Sudetenland. Six months later, in March 1939, Nazi troops marched into what was left of Czechoslovakia and seized control.

WORLD WAR II

World War II affected virtually every part of the world from 1939 to 1945. This time the sides were broken down into the Axis powers—Germany, Italy, and Japan—and the Allied forces—France, Great Britain, the United States, the Soviet Union, and China. Many of the reasons for the war were the

A Czech woman salutes Nazi troops as they march into Czechoslovakia during World War II.

GYPSIES AND THE *PORAJMOS*

It wasn't only the Jews of Europe who were sent to death camps by the Nazis. Approximately 250,000 to 500,000 Romanies (Gypsies or Roma) were systematically registered, ghettoized, and then deported to concentration camps during the Holocaust as well. The word the Roma use for the Holocaust is *Porajmos*, which means "Devouring."

It is now believed that the Roma originally migrated from northern India approximately one thousand years ago and dispersed throughout Europe over the next several centuries. They were given the name "Gypsies" during the Middle Ages when many Europeans believed that they had come from Egypt.

The Nazis were not the first to try to eliminate the Gypsies. For centuries, many people throughout Europe tried to force the Roma to give up their culture; others tried to force them to move elsewhere. Attempts to assimilate them included giving them land and cattle, with the expectation that they would give up their nomadic lifestyle and become farmers, and stealing their children so they could grow up with non-Roma families. Laws were passed outlawing Roma customs, language, and clothing. Not even Joseph II was enlightened enough to include the Roma in the list of peoples whose religious beliefs should be protected.

same as those that had prompted World War I: social unrest, economic depression, national aggression, religious and ethnic intolerance, and territorial disputes. Humiliated by their defeat in the last war and devastated by years of economic depression, many Germans supported Hitler's philosophy of Aryan supremacy and his plans to rearm Germany and reclaim the role of superpower. They made him dictator and gave him unlimited power.

Hitler knew that other European leaders were still so devastated by the horrors of the last war that they would go to great lengths to avoid another one. He counted on that as he systematically invaded and then took over the neighboring European countries of Poland, Czechoslovakia, Slovakia, Hungary, Romania, Bulgaria, Belgium, Holland, and France. He allied himself with two other Fascist dictators, Italy's Benito Mussolini, and Japan's Emperor Hirohito.

In all of the countries the Nazis occupied, citizens risked their lives to form underground resistance movements. As it had during World War I, the Czech resistance movement found a lot of support from Czech expatriates who were living overseas. The

*Edvard Benes fled
Czechoslovakia when
the Nazis invaded. He
became the leader of
the provisional Czech
government.*

former Czech president, Edvard Benes, had managed to flee to
Britain when the Nazis invaded in 1939. In 1940 he persuaded
the British government to officially recognize him as the leader
of the provisional "free Czechoslovak government-in-exile." In
turn, he persuaded many Czechs living in Britain to enlist in the
British armed forces and help in the fight against Hitler. Anti-
German Czechoslovak army units were formed in France, the
United States, and North Africa.

Czechs quickly learned that they would pay dearly for their
efforts to resist the Nazis. Seven months after Hitler's troops invaded Czechoslovakia, in October 1939, crowds of Czechs

LIQUIDATION OF LIDICE

In 1942, Czech subversives managed to assassinate Reinhard Heydrich, the supreme commander of Nazi troops in Czechoslovakia during Hitler's occupation. A mastermind of Nazi genocide, Heydrich was the highest-ranking Nazi to be assassinated during the war. Hitler retaliated against the Czech people by ordering Lidice, a small village which had had nothing to do with the assassination plot, to be completely destroyed. Nazi troops immediately murdered all 192 men of the town and sent all women and children by train to the Ravensbrück concentration camp, where most were gassed to death within days of their arrival. Of the entire town, only sixteen children survived and were eventually rescued from the camps at the end of the war. As horrifying as these acts were, Hitler went even further to ensure that the Czechs clearly understood what would happen if there were further resistance attempts. He ordered Nazi soldiers to level all the town's buildings. The area where Lidice once stood remains today exactly as the Nazis left it. The Czechs have carefully preserved the site as both a memorial to the people of Lidice and a lasting symbol of Nazi barbarism.

Nazi soldiers set fire to buildings in Lidice.

gathered in the streets of Prague to commemorate an event they had proudly celebrated every October for the last twenty-one years: their independence as a nation. This year there was little to celebrate. Instead, the gathering turned into an angry mob of protest against the German occupation. The Nazis wasted no time in retaliating. They immediately arrested nine students on charges of organizing the protest demonstration and sentenced them all to death. Then they closed all the Czech universities and sent twelve hundred university students to labor camps.

Stunned by the Nazi brutality, members of the Czech and Slovak resistance stopped demonstrating in public and went underground, turning to methods of sabotage instead of public protest. On May 27, 1942, they assassinated Reinhard Heydrich, the acting German governor of Bohemia and Moravia. Again, the Nazis responded with swift brutality. Nazi troops conducted relentless house-to-house searches, arresting anyone they even remotely suspected of being a member of the Czech resistance. Within days, they executed more than sixteen hundred Czechs and sent thousands more to concentration camps. They got the effect they wanted: The resistance movement was squashed.

Until the war ended in 1945, Czechs lived their daily lives under the iron-fisted control of Nazi totalitarianism. When the Germans lost the war, other nations who suffered under Nazi

CZECH NAZI LABOR CAMP VICTIMS TO RECEIVE 423 MILLION DEUTSCHE MARKS (DM)

In early 2001 a conference was held in Berlin to agree on compensation to be paid to the millions of people who were forced to work as slave laborers for Nazi Germany during World War II. The agreement was signed by representatives from Germany, the United States, and Israel, as well as the Czech Republic, Poland, Hungary, and other former Eastern bloc nations. The countries agreed that DM 10 billion (approximately U.S. $466,408,820) will be allocated to victims worldwide. DM 423 million of that sum (approximately U.S. $197,290,931) has been allocated to compensate Czechs who were forced into slave labor. German chancellor Gerhard Schroeder stated that "with this agreement we can close the last open chapter of the past." Not everyone is satisfied with this settlement. Most of the Czech laborers who are still alive after all these years are aged and feel that the $7,000 that each can now expect to receive is unfair and inadequate.

rule were liberated by the Allied forces of France, Great Britain, and the United States, and these nations were eventually allowed to reconstruct their own independent national governments. Unfortunately for the Czechs, Slovaks, and several other Eastern European countries, however, liberation meant trading one totalitarian regime for another. Forty years of repression under the Communists were yet to come.

4 COMMUNIST CONTROL

As they had so many times before, Czech lands became a political football in Europe's postwar power struggles. This time, the contending parties included the rising superpowers of the United States and the Union of Soviet Socialist Republics. There was no bloody war of open aggression, but instead a "cold" war of political propaganda, threats, intimidation, and the stockpiling of nuclear weapons. But the stakes were just as high and the tension just as riveting.

THE COLD WAR

On February 11, 1945, U.S. president Franklin D. Roosevelt, USSR premier Joseph Stalin, and British prime minister Winston Churchill met at the Yalta Conference in Crimea to plan the final defeat of Nazi Germany. They agreed that after the war ended, Germany and the territories it had conquered would be divided into occupied zones, each to be administered by U.S., British, French, or Soviet forces. The three leaders agreed that Czechoslovakia would be liberated by the Soviet Red Army marching in from the east and that Czechoslovakia would then come under the Soviet sphere of influence after the end of the war. In May 1945, within days after the Soviets entered Czechoslovakia, Germany unconditionally surrendered to Allied forces and the war in Europe was over.

The cold war developed almost immediately after World War II ended with a rivalry between two former allies: the United States and the Soviet Union. By 1948 the Soviets had installed Communist governments in Czechoslovakia and the other countries of Eastern Europe that had been liberated by the Red Army. Control over these governments was maintained by the head of the USSR and the Soviet Communist Party, Joseph Stalin. In addition to spreading their Communist ideology, the Soviets wanted a strong coalition of Eastern bloc nations as a safeguard against another rise of German power. For their part, the United States and its European allies were afraid that the

Soviet Communists would not stop with Eastern Europe and would try to take over the rest of the world.

The United States was disturbed by its view of Eastern Europe being held against its will by the Soviets. But Czechoslovakia did not become a Communist state simply because it was absorbed into the USSR's sphere of influence. Czechs did not view Communism as a repressive, totalitarian form of government. During World War II many Czechs had been so repulsed by the right-wing politics of Nazi Fascism that they leaned heavily to the left, embracing Socialist and Communist ideologies that valued the common laborer. Even though it consisted mostly of Communist officials, the first postwar government of Czechoslovakia was actually an elected one.

The Czech Communist Party had strong political and ideological ties to Moscow. Once the party's members were elected to key political positions, the Soviets pressured them to systematically take over other parts of the government until, by

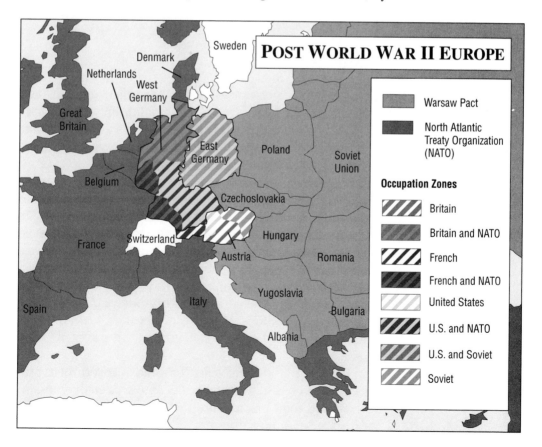

POST WORLD WAR II EUROPE

REINVENTING HISTORY

For hundreds of years, occupying tyrants have psychologically manipulated Czechs by rewriting history and renaming geography. Czech writer Milan Kundera described how unsettling this could be in his novels about totalitarian repression. In his novel *The Book of Laughter and Forgetting,* he writes: "The street Tamina was born on was called Schwerin. That was during the war when the Germans occupied Prague. Her father was born on Cernokostelecka Avenue—the Avenue of the Black Church. That was during the Austro-Hungarian Monarchy. When her mother married her father and moved there, it bore the name of Marshal Foch. That was after World War I. Tamina spent her childhood on Stalin Avenue, and when her husband came to take her away, he went to Vinohrady—that is, Vineyards—Avenue. And all the time it was the same street; they just kept changing its name, trying to lobotomize it. There are all kinds of ghosts prowling these confused streets. They are the ghosts of monuments demolished—demolished by the Czech Reformation, demolished by the Austrian Counterreformation, demolished by the Czechoslovak Republic, demolished by the Communists. Even statues of Stalin have been torn down. All over the country, wherever statues were thus destroyed, Lenin statues have sprouted up by the thousands. They grow like weeds on the ruins, like melancholy flowers of forgetting."

the end of 1947, they controlled the Ministry of Defense, the armed forces, and most law enforcement agencies. President Edvard Benes was not strong enough politically to stop them, nor were any of Czechoslovakia's other political parties. None had enough power on their own and they couldn't agree enough to unite against the stronger, more organized Communist Party.

The Communists soon demanded that Benes officially replace the democratic government with a Communist one. On February 25, 1948, Benes complied. One hour later, even though Benes was technically still president, Communist leader Klement Gottwald appeared in front of a cheering crowd on Old Town Square to announce his party's victory. He had reason to celebrate. For the next forty-one years, the Czech Communist Party (directed by Moscow) would have complete political, social, and economic control over the lives of Czech citizens.

In October of the same year, Communist government officials forced Benes to nationalize the country's coal mines, industrial and food production plants, banks, and insurance companies. Nationalizing meant that the businesses were taken away from private individuals and given to the state to own and run. More than three thousand companies were nationalized, and that was just the beginning.

THE "SOCIALIZATION" OF CZECHOSLOVAKIA

As soon as they took control of the government, the Communists halted any kind of democratic procedures that could undermine their power. When elections were held that year, the only candidates Czech voters could choose from were certified members of the Communist Party. Anyone who tried to campaign who wasn't a party member was arrested. When voters expressed their anger by not voting at all, the government falsified the election results, claiming that more than 90 percent of the population had voted their resounding support for Communist leadership.

But even these measures didn't satisfy the Communist Party, who wanted their leadership guaranteed by the country's constitution. So the Communist-controlled parliament passed a

Many Czech citizens joined the Communist Party during Soviet rule.

new constitution that ensured that the Communist Party would always play the "leading role" in Czech government. That was too much for Benes, who refused to sign the new legislation. His refusal did not bother the Communist Party because they had needed his heroic reputation as a Czech nationalist only to mollify the people until the transition to Communist control was complete. Benes was forced to resign and was immediately replaced by Antonín Zápotocký, a high-ranking Communist.

A week later, parliament passed even more legislation to guarantee that Communists would remain in control. They nationalized all the midsized, privately owned Czech companies that hadn't been nationalized earlier. By the end of 1948, 95 percent of the workforce in Czechoslovakia worked for the state.

Socialist posters on a billboard in Prague in 1955 illustrate the Communist presence in Czechoslovakia.

The next year, small tradesmen and shopkeepers lost their businesses to the state as well. By the end of 1949 parliament even nationalized Czech agriculture with a law that replaced all private farms with state-owned collectives.

Anyone who protested the new economic and political system faced serious consequences. People who openly criticized party policy were now not only forbidden from running for political office, but they were also arrested and prosecuted as enemies of the state. Communist Party leaders in Moscow sent advisers to teach Czech officials how to track down anti-Communist subversives. The most effective way to deal with them, they advised, was to inter them in forced labor camps. Between 1949 and 1953, hundreds of thousands of suspected subversives were forced into years, sometimes even decades, of hard labor at camps like the notorious Jáchymov uranium mines.

What was most terrifying to Czechs about this type of persecution was that the most mundane action could be construed as anti-Communist even if it weren't in any way meant as criticism of the government or Communist Party. For example, people who were caught listening to rock and roll music on foreign radio stations like Radio Netherlands were considered subversives and were jailed. Reading books, watching movies, or viewing art that was not approved by the Communists was forbidden. People were encouraged to contact authorities if they felt that their coworkers, friends, and even family members were engaging in potentially subversive activities, including reading subversive material. Often, little or no proof of the accusations was needed. Suspicion alone was enough to have someone arrested.

Because of the sagging economy under Communist rule, Czech morale plummeted. State law decreed that every adult man and woman must hold a job. Yet, because the government owned all business and industry, it controlled salaries and working conditions. By 1953, despite the consequences of such actions, people staged anti-Communist protests in an effort to inspire other workers to their cause. The government responded with a new tactic: Not only were the protesters removed to forced labor camps, but the government also ordered that all future references to the incidents—and to many of the people who participated in them—be erased. The protest never happened; the people never existed. Rewriting the events of history became a frightening and powerful psychological tool of the Communist government.

President Antonín Novotný changed his country's name to the Czechoslovak Socialist Republic.

In May 1955 the Soviet Union officially declared its power over Czechoslovakia and the other Eastern bloc countries: Bulgaria, Hungary, Poland, Romania, and Albania became "satellites" of the Soviet Union, united by a "Treaty of Friendship, Cooperation and Mutual Assistance" called the Warsaw Pact.[3] The Warsaw Pact was a military alliance that protected the Soviet empire from its enemies in the West, particularly against the North Atlantic Treaty Organization (NATO) that the United States, France, Britain, and other Western European nations had formed after the end of World War II. The Warsaw Pact was originally intended to last for only twenty years, but did not end until the dissolution of the USSR in 1991.

After the death of President Antonín Zápotocký, another high-ranking Communist, Antonín Novotný, was officially elected president. Under his rule, the country adopted a new name to reflect its status as a satellite of the USSR: The Czechoslovak Socialist Republic (CSSR). Neither its new name nor its new status helped the Czech economy. And neither the economy nor the spirit of the Czech people would brighten again until the late 1960s.

THE PRAGUE SPRING

For the next thirteen years, the Czechs became increasingly angry with the oppressive Communist rule and afraid that the already depressed economy would get even worse. The old guard of Communist leaders throughout the Soviet Union did not respond to the growing unrest or even acknowledge it. Younger party members who were rising through the ranks started to realize that Communism would not be able to hold on to its power if it didn't admit that change was needed. One of the first of these leaders, Alexander Dubcek, came to power in Czechoslovakia in January 1968.

As soon as he was named first secretary of the Communist Party of Czechoslovakia, Dubcek made public speeches admitting that some aspects of Communism were not working. When he publicly admitted that the Communist Party had sometimes gone too far in its use of political harassment and that its own industrial and agricultural policies had made a mess of the economy, he definitely got peoples' attention.

Dubcek promised changes and he delivered them. He said the government would stop persecuting people for their political convictions and would recognize basic human rights and liberties. Working conditions in industries and on farms improved when the government began rewarding people for working harder and for devising more efficient ways to produce and ship their products. Foreign trade was opened up, which raised prices and salaries. Writers, musicians, and artists were allowed to create their art without government censorship, and it was no longer illegal to read or view formerly banned literature and art from Western countries. Czech culture blossomed

THE DUBIOUS DEATH OF ALEXANDER DUBCEK

Alexander Dubcek died in 1992, more than twenty years after Moscow ordered his resignation as the leader of Czechoslovakia. Even so, his death produced wild rumors of murder and conspiracy. Although Dubcek had been a decorated war hero and remained a staunch defender of the Communist Party, the reforms he initiated in the Prague Spring of 1968 earned him almost fifteen years of hard labor in the Slovak forestry service.

The official cause of his death was a car crash, but that did not stop an older generation of Czechs from speculating that the Soviet or Czechoslovak secret police had finally avenged their old hatreds and murdered him. For years, the investigation into his death remained open as people voiced absurd conspiracy theories. Some Slovakian leftists were sure that Slovakia's nationalist federal prime minister, Vladimir Meciar, had Dubcek killed because Dubcek had been opposed to splitting up Czechoslovakia into the Czech and Slovak Republics, and that even after years away from politics, Dubcek was somehow still powerful enough to reunite the two countries. Others said Meciar had him murdered because Dubcek was blackmailing him. Some people went so far as to claim that Czech president Václav Havel had ordered the hit because he was afraid of Dubcek's potential political power.

After years of investigation, Slovak officials reviewed the reports and concluded that Dubcek's death was not a political assassination. It was just what it appeared to be: a tragic accident caused by a chauffeur who had driven too fast in a heavy rainstorm and skidded off the road. Still, some people remain convinced that Dubcek's death involved foul play.

and its own art and literature drew international attention. It was no longer illegal to listen to Western music. Rock clubs sprang up, hippie culture flourished, and even miniskirts became acceptable.

But in spite of the freedoms and radical government reforms Dubcek advocated, he still considered himself a loyal Communist. He wholeheartedly believed that Communism was the best social, political, and economic system, but that it needed to be modernized. Dubcek called his reforms an attempt to create "socialism with a human face."[4] To the Czech people, his efforts in the late 1960s created an exciting and promising new era they called the "Prague Spring."

FORCED NORMALIZATION

Alexander Dubcek carried out reforms that allowed Czech culture and the economy to prosper.

The Czechs may have been delighted with Dubcek's reforms, but Communist Party officials back in Moscow were appalled. The Soviet Union saw Dubcek's changes as a major threat to its control over its satellite nations. Soviet leaders openly criticized Dubcek and repeatedly warned him and the people of Czechoslovakia to put a stop to the reforms or face serious consequences. Neither Dubcek nor the Czechoslovaks realized just how serious those consequences would be.

On August 20, 1968, the Soviet Union sent forces in armored tanks to invade Czechoslovakia. The news footage the next morning of tanks rolling through the streets of Prague stunned the world. The Soviets justified their invasion by insisting that loyal Czech Communists had demanded their help in putting down what they saw as a dangerous revolution that threatened the existence of the Communist way of life in Eastern Europe. Alexander Dubcek was called to Moscow and promptly fired, both from political office and from the Communist Party. He was replaced with a hard-line Communist Party member named Gustav Husák. Under orders from Soviet leaders, Husák instituted a new policy

Armored Soviet tanks rolled across Czechoslovakia in 1968 to quell the cultural revolution called the "Prague Spring."

for Czechoslovakia, which he called "normalization." It was an innocent-sounding word for a policy that was even more harsh and repressive than pre-Dubcek Communism had been. Normalization would last for the next twenty years.

Regardless of the harsh crackdown, Czechs did not easily give up on the idea of freedom. More than 150,000 Czechs and Slovaks had managed to flee across Czechoslovakia's borders to political sanctuary in the West. Many of these people wrote articles and books and conducted interviews with the Western media to make sure the world did not forget the plight of their countrymen and -women. As they had done during both World

A woman mourns the death of Jan Palach, a student who set himself on fire to protest Communist rule in Czechoslovakia.

War I and II, Czechs organized a supportive resistance movement. Many of those who stayed continued to risk years in prison and labor camps to carry out anti-Soviet demonstrations. They, too, did what they could to attract international media attention. One of the more well known incidents occurred in January 1969, when Jan Palach, a young university student in Prague, immolated himself (set himself on fire) during a protest demonstration.

By early 1970 thousands of suspected anti-Communists had been sent to labor camps. Half a million more were permanently expelled from the Communist Party. Losing one's status as a party member could have a devastating effect on a family when one or both of the breadwinners were professionals such as doctors, lawyers, scientists, engineers, or teachers. Only party members were allowed to hold jobs in almost every profession. Because it was illegal to be unemployed, professionally trained people who lost their party status were forced to spend the rest of their lives working at low-paying, menial jobs such as washing windows or collecting garbage. No one knew that harsh fact of Communist life better than Dubcek himself. He ended up spending the next twenty years after his demotion doing forestry work in the Slovak Mountains.

Resistance continued to grow in the 1970s and 1980s, especially on university campuses. A whole new generation of activists emerged. They continued to stage provocative protest demonstrations that caught international media attention. Many were poets, artists, novelists, and playwrights who used their art to vividly portray what life was like under Communism. Some did get their works published within Czechoslovakia, but most were heavily censored or banned altogether. That didn't stop collaborators from helping smuggle the works out of the country to widespread, enthusiastic audiences in the West, especially Germany, Great Britian, and the United States. One of these influential anti-Communist writers was Václav Havel, whose plays satirized Communist bureaucrats and the devastating effect they had on every aspect of Czech life.

Political activism and unrest were also rising in other satellite nations as well as within the Soviet Union itself. The Communist economy throughout the Eastern bloc was in shambles; industry and technology were outdated, and agriculture hopelessly inefficient. The standard of living for most people was extremely low. Housing was cramped and there were waiting lists for apartments as well as for appliances and other consumer goods. Salaries and working conditions were terrible; morale was worse. For four decades the United States and other Western nations had convinced themselves that the spread of Communism could be stopped by keeping nuclear missiles trained on Soviet sites, unaware that years of bad economic policies, party corruption, and the misuse of power had disintegrated the system from within.

THE VELVET REVOLUTION

Dubcek may have been the first Communist leader to realize that social, economic, and political reforms were badly needed, but he was not the only one. During the second half of the

VÁCLAV HAVEL, PLAYWRIGHT AND REVOLUTIONARY

Václav Havel, Czech writer, revolutionary, and politician, will no doubt be remembered as one of the leading figures in Czech history. He was born in October 1936, the son of a prominent Prague businessman. Havel graduated with a degree in economics in 1957 from the Czech Technical University, but his real interest was the theater. He enrolled in the Academy of Performing Arts for another four years, to study drama. After serving his compulsory tour of duty in the Czech army, he was hired by one of Prague's largest theaters, first as a stagehand, later as an assistant director, and then as the director of plays he wrote himself. One of his first plays, *The Garden Party*, produced in 1963, brought him international acclaim.

Havel wrote experimental, absurdist plays that depicted the horrors of life in a totalitarian society. Many of his early plays were written during the Prague Spring, at a time when censorship in Czechoslovakia was loosened. After the Soviets invaded Czechoslovakia in 1968 and reimposed harsh censorship laws, Havel's works were banned in his own country. In response, Havel became a radical and outspoken political dissident. His illegal political activities, which included hosting concerts of banned music in his country cottage, got him arrested a number of times and imprisoned twice. In 1977 he published his famous Charter 77, a human rights initiative that protested the oppression of Czechs by the Communist government. That led to even greater political involvement as Havel became the principal spokesperson for two groups: the Civic Forum, a pro-independence group that evolved out of Charter 77, and the Committee for the Defense of the Unjustly Prosecuted. At the same time, he continued writing controversial plays, including *Largo Desolato* (1984) and *Slum Clearance* (1987), and stirring political essays. He was also active in the Czechoslovak underground press.

In 1989, the Civic Forum succeeded in forcing the Communist Party to share power and appointed Havel interim president of Czechoslovakia. In 1990, he was officially elected to a two-year term as president. He opposed the breakup of Czechoslovakia into the Czech and Slovak Republics and resigned in 1992 when parliament approved it. He was elected the first president of the new Czech Republic in 1993 and was still in office in 2001.

1980s Soviet leader Mikhail Gorbachev initiated some reforms of his own. He publicly referred to these reforms as perestroika, defined as "deep transformations in the economy and the whole system of social relations."[5]

Like Dubcek before him, Gorbachev believed that government should be less repressive of people's rights. He believed the economy would only improve if people had a greater say in how their state-controlled workplaces were run and if they were rewarded more for hard work. And like Dubcek, Gorbachev was a staunch Communist whose intention was not to undermine the Communist system of government, but rather to put into action a series of controlled reforms that would make the government—and therefore the country—run more efficiently. With less censorship and hopes of a better economy, he believed, the Soviet people would work harder to help the USSR catch up to Western technological advances.

Gorbacev was not blind to the ongoing unrest in Czechoslovakia and the Soviet Union's other satellite countries. But he feared that he would not be able to control the effect of perestroika in these areas, and that it might lead to outright anti-Communist rebellion. So he limited his reforms to the Soviet Union. Czech activists were outraged when they learned that the reforms they wanted were being initiated in the Soviet Union but not in Czechoslovakia. They increased the number and intensity of their political demonstrations against President Husák and his hard-line Communist rule, demanding that reforms be made in their country, too. Protesters demonstrated throughout the Soviet satellite nations, including East Germany.

In November 1989 the world cheered an unprecedented act of protest—the tearing down of the Berlin Wall. In 1961 Soviets had built the wall out of concrete and barbed wire to keep the people of East Berlin from escaping to West Berlin. It immediately became a vivid symbol of Communist tyranny. The fall of the Berlin Wall marked the end of Communist control of East Germany and increased the fervor of Czech protests, but symbolically it was the beginning of the end for the Soviet Union itself. It took only another month and a half to topple the Communist regime in Czechoslovakia as well.

The six-week period between November 17 and December 29, 1989, became known worldwide as the Velvet Revolution because there was almost no violence in the overthrow of Communist rule. The Czechs themselves refer to those weeks as "the November events."

The exact date the revolution began, November 17, 1989, was the fiftieth anniversary of the funeral of Jan Upletal, a university student who was gunned down in Prague on November 13, 1939, during a rally to protest the Nazi occupation of Czechoslovakia. A gathering to commemorate Upletal turned into a protest against Communist rule. Even after the government called in riot police to break up the demonstrations, the protesters—mostly university students—tried to keep the confrontation nonviolent. Instead of fighting back against the police, the students offered them flowers. Nevertheless, in a short time, the police had seriously injured more than 160 demonstrators.

The police action rallied more Czech people to the students' revolutionary cause. Organized by dissident leaders such as Václav Havel, workers unions began staging mass solidarity demonstrations throughout the country. Havel and several other activist leaders formed the Civic Forum, an organization whose first official act was to demand the resignation of the Communist government, the release of all imprisoned dissidents, and investigations into the November 17 police action. A similar movement was initiated called the Public Against Violence. Within weeks, both movements comprised students, factory workers, professional people, and even farmers. The newspaper, radio, and television

A protester waves the Czech flag during a 1989 demonstration in Prague.

media disregarded government censorship and began issuing reports throughout the country and, when possible, abroad about the movement.

Communist Party leaders back in Moscow were overwhelmed with the recent events in East Germany and were unprepared to deal with Czechoslovakia. The Czechoslovak Communist Party Central Committee did their best to head off a revolution of their own. Hoping more powerful leadership would help quell the turmoil, they called a special meeting in which they elected a new party head, Karel Urbanek. They tried to stop further anti-Communist demontrations and stall for time until they could get stronger backing from Moscow by promising to put through legislative reforms. But their meaningless promises did not fool the Czech people. When the Civic Forum rejected their offers, Urbanek and other government leaders were forced to hold talks with Haval and other leaders of the Civic Forum, in which they agreed to form a new coalition government with a parliament that included non-Communists. The new parliament's first official act was to elect Václav Havel as president of Czechoslovakia.

A supporter carries a poster of Václav Havel, the playwright and reformer who brought an end to Soviet rule.

An amazed world watched as fifty years of repression and terror under first the Nazis and then the Communists ended in a peaceful transfer of power to democratic rule. Within months, free elections were held. Although democratic law allowed the Communist Party to continue to exist, the Czech people rejected Communism in almost every local and national political race.

THE CZECH REPUBLIC IN THE 1990S

The changes the country experienced during that first decade of democracy were difficult and often overwhelming. Czechs and Slovaks realized that they had more differences than goals in common. Although they both wanted to replace Communism with a working democracy, they neither could agree on the timing of economic reforms nor even how radical the reforms should be. Because of these differing opinions, a nationwide referendum was held in December 1992, in which the people

FORUM 2000

Because of its history, no country knows better than the Czech Republic that politics, economics, and humanitarian issues have to be addressed on an international level. To promote an open dialogue among the world's humanitarians, politicians, diplomats, and commentators, the Czech Republic hosted an international conference called Forum 2000.

The three-day event was led jointly by President Václav Havel and Elie Wiesel, the writer and Holocaust survivor who won the Nobel Peace Prize in 1986. For three days, more than sixty participants met in Prague to exchange ideas. Ten of the distinguished attendees were Nobel laureates, including Shimon Peres, former prime minister of Israel and one of the architects of the Oslo Peace Accord; F. W. de Klerk, the former president of South Africa who helped negotiate the end of apartheid; Richard von Weizsäcker, the former German president who helped coordinate the reunification of Germany; Crown Prince Hassan of Jordan; and the Dalai Lama, the Buddhist spiritual leader. The conference also included newsman Ted Koppel, adventurer and archaeologist Thor Heyerdahl, as well as human rights activists, writers, philosophers, and professors from around the world.

The speeches and dialogues went beyond thrashing current political issues. The focus of the conference was to find ways for nations to work together in the future to protect human rights, promote the health and education of children, save the environment, and learn to respect each other's ethnic heritages and spiritual views.

voted to dissolve the nation of Czechoslovakia. The result was two individual nations: the Czech and Slovak Republics, which have since maintained a friendly relationship.

Czechs were faced with the daunting prospect of having to re-create not just a whole new government, but also a blueprint for a new economy. During the first few years when legislators struggled with this challenge, banks and businesses failed and unemployment soared. Not everyone had the country's best interests at heart. Corrupt politicians got rich on bribes from unscrupulous businessmen. Meanwhile, other problems, including crime and pollution, were not being addressed. But the Czechs themselves never lost their determination to re-create a new government and economy. At the beginning of the twenty-first century, although many problems linger, that determination is finally beginning to bring results.

Modern Life in the Czech Republic

The Velvet Revolution and the end of Communism in 1989 changed a lot more than the structure of the government and ownership of industry; it changed many aspects of daily Czech life, including family, work, education, and leisure. Censorship restrictions were lifted on television and radio programming, newspapers, and book publishing. Western pop culture flooded the country and influenced everything from the kind of music many Czechs enjoyed to the way they shopped for food and clothing. Technological advances revolutionized communications, transportation, and industry. Capitalism fostered a desire for more material goods. Yet at the same time, other, more traditional aspects of Czech life remain as they have for decades, even centuries.

An Ethnic Mix of People

One constant is the diverse ethnic mix of the Czech population, which has remained essentially the same since the Velvet Revolution. Of the approximately 11 million people in the Czech Republic, about 81 percent are Czechs, 13 percent Moravians, and 3 percent are Slovaks, with smaller minorities of Germans, Poles, and Romanies (also known as Gypsies). A small Vietnamese minority also exists. Originally invited into the country as guest workers, they stayed to raise families and became Czech citizens. Unfortunately, another of the constants of the Czech population is discrimination against the smaller minorities, especially the Romanies, who have been the target of hatred for centuries due to their very different language, customs, and beliefs.

Czechs as a whole do not consider themselves very religious. The religion claiming largest membership (with slightly fewer than 40 percent of the Czech population) is the Roman Catholic Church, but even a large number of self-proclaimed Catholics say they do not attend services on a regular basis. The same is

A Prague synagogue offers a place of worship for the city's Jewish population.

true for the next-largest religion, the Hussite Church. There are also a number of Protestant Christian denominations, such as the Evangelical Church of Czech Brethren. The Jewish population, which was radically diminished during the Nazi occupation, is a tiny minority today. Prague has the largest Jewish community in the Republic, with about six thousand members, although Jewish communities also thrive in other large cities such as Ostrava and Brno.

MAKING A LIVING

Regardless of their religious beliefs, ethnic backgrounds, or even their political affiliations, the biggest change the Czech people experienced in the second half of the twentieth century was the move away from a primarily agrarian (farming) economy. The majority of Czechs now live in cities rather than in rural areas, and a large number of those who do live outside of urban areas are employed not as farmers but as miners, forestry service employees, and workers in electrical and nuclear energy plants.

People in urban areas work in a wild variety of industries, including textiles, leather products, furniture, chemicals, rubber, plastics, china, paper, petroleum, and industrial and farm machinery. After the dissolution of the Soviet Union, and the subsequent lifting of travel restrictions, tourism quickly became a successful industry, employing many Czechs in its growing number of hotels, restaurants, resorts, and spas. An increasing number of people are involved in computer jobs, designing and processing information and communications systems. Since the 1990s many high-tech companies have recruited thousands of computer experts from the United States and Europe to help the Czech Republic keep pace with rapid technological advancements.

URBAN CHALLENGES

Although unemployment is still relatively high and a majority of the country's available jobs are in urban areas, few people migrate from rural towns to larger cities in search of jobs because of the scarcity of affordable housing. The Communist government tried to relieve the housing shortage in the 1960s and 1970s by building sprawling concrete apartment complexes on the outskirts of

Increased travel opportunities to the Czech Republic have resulted in more jobs in the hotel and restaurant industry.

Czech cities. Today the housing shortage is so dire that many families have little choice but to live in these ugly, unlandscaped, and often crumbling apartment blocks. Even the more modern and expensive apartments are cramped for families with in-laws and children, and city dwellers who can afford it often buy or rent small cottages in the country where they spend their weekends and vacations.

Besides a shortage of housing, Czech cities have other serious problems, including traffic congestion, air pollution, and crime. Although the government has spent millions making public transportation such as train, bus, and subway lines cheap and reliable, more Czechs can now afford to buy cars. Cars have long been a status symbol in the Czech Republic. During the Communist era, when almost all material goods including cars and household appliances manufactured in Soviet countries were scarce and imports were not allowed from the West, large deposits were required for cars, and the wait for delivery often lasted years.

Since the fall of Communism, new and used cars have become easier to import and hundreds of thousands more are produced by the country's own car brand, Skoda, which is owned by Volkswagen. Even though cars are very expensive—gasoline averages $3 per gallon, and it can cost almost as much to park a car per month as rent an apartment—automobile sales continue to escalate. The narrow, twisting streets of cities built hundreds of years ago cannot accommodate the flow of traffic, and exhaust fumes on some days greatly diminish air quality, but it is not likely that Czechs will give up their car craze any time soon.

EDUCATION

Education has changed drastically since the fall of Communism. Children between the ages of six and sixteen are still required by law to attend school, but parents now have the choice of sending them to private schools. Under Communism only state-run schools with strictly censored teaching materials and subjects taught from a hard-line Communist perspective existed. Today public schools still exist, but parents help determine what is taught and by whom.

The most dramatic change in education is that Communist history and philosophy are no longer mandatory subjects. Before 1989 this indoctrination was considered so important that a student who failed complex state exams about Communism

University students (pictured) pay no tuition but must pass difficult entrance exams.

was not eligible for a university degree, regardless of how knowledgeable that student was in medicine, law, science, or other subjects. Under Communism, because Czechoslovakia was a Soviet satellite, the Russian language was also a compulsory subject throughout grade school and high school. Although Russian is still an important language today and many students choose it for their mandatory second language, children have a wider range of languages to choose from and often opt to learn a Western language such as German, English, or French.

Like many of the other extensive changes in the Czech Republic since the 1990s, the changeover to the new, non-Communist education system has been expensive. Teachers at all grade levels have had to be retrained. Textbooks have had to be rewritten or, more often, replaced entirely. Entire libraries have had to be updated. With the demand for more foreign languages, school systems now also often hire German, French, and English teachers to teach their native languages in Czech schools.

Czech children attend grade school for five years, until the age of eleven. After completing grade school—and based on exams and the students' own interests—a decision is made between three different tracks of secondary school study: academic (preparation for college), technical (training for electrical, carpentry, or computer-related occupations, for example), and teaching. University students do not pay tuition, but they must have good grades and do well on entry exams. University studies are no longer the only post–secondary school educational opportunity. An increasing number of students who graduate on the technical secondary track can now enroll in advanced two-year training programs for additional degrees. Students who choose the teaching track go on to special teaching colleges.

Despite the changes in education, economy, and urban life brought about after the fall of Communism, other, more traditional aspects of Czech life have remained constant, such as the importance of family ties, love of hearty food, indulgence in leisure pursuits, and celebration of holiday festivities.

FAMILY LIFE

Throughout their troubled history Czech families have been close and tightly knit. Urban families are usually small, rarely with more than two children. Rural families are often larger, mainly because they have more living space to accommodate the extra people and because children are needed to help with farming. Whether rural or urban, both parents usually work full time outside the home. Although gender roles are beginning to change, women are the hardest hit because they are also usually responsible for maintaining the household and raising the children.

Czechs usually marry by their mid- to late twenties, after they are out of school and on their way to developing careers. Until then, however, many continue living with their parents, mainly because housing is so scarce and expensive. If parents have the room, young couples might spend the first few years of married life with them as well. Most people get married in civil ceremonies, although an increasing number are choosing to hold an additional ceremony in a church or synagogue.

CZECH CUISINE

Czech appetites have changed little over the years, and traditional Czech cuisine is considered hearty and delicious, but not exactly healthful. A popular nineteenth-century Czech novelist—Ignat Hermann—vividly described the eating habits of one of his characters, a typical Czech family man. Breakfast might be a heaping plate of bacon and eggs, followed by an equally calorie-laden lunch: a platter of hot sausages with homemade rolls and mustard, grated horseradish, and a bowl of pickles, accompanied by a stein or two of hearty Czech beer. Dinner was usually the heaviest meal of the day, consisting of a main meat course such as veal rolls with pork stuffing or roasted wild venison, accompanied by

REAWAKENING THE CZECH FEMINIST MOVEMENT

In July 2000, the International Helsinki Foundation released its Survey on the Status of Women in the Czech Republic. The report found that although Czech women comprise 44 percent of the work force, their unemployment rate is almost twice that of men, and their earnings are only 70 percent of men's. Women also hold most of the low-paying jobs. The survey also reported that while most Czech women hold full-time jobs, they are still responsible for taking care of their homes and children. Czech women are only too aware of these statistics and have become increasingly organized in their efforts to create change.

Feminism is not a new phenomenon in Czech history. Women have actively participated in the major events of Czech history, especially during the Hussite movement and the Czech National Revival. The Hussites emphasized equality and believed that everyone (both men and women) should be educated at least well enough to read the Bible. Equality was an even greater factor during the cultural awakening of the nineteenth-century Czech National Revival. At that time, both men and women were encouraged to persue university educations because the revivalists wanted as many writers, artists, and composers as possible to breathe new life into Czech culture and language.

The Communists claimed to be pro-feminist, too. When the Communist Party took over the country in 1948, they started a massive propaganda campaign to induce both men and women to become workers in the state-run industries and followers of Communist Party philosophy. The propaganda was designed to give women the illusion of emancipation. The Communist state valued them (it claimed) because they were physically and intellectually capable of working in any occupation, of being active politically and socially, and still being able to function as good wives and mothers.

In actuality, of course, women were required to work full-time jobs, whether they wanted to or not. Anyone who didn't was breaking the law and thrown into prison. That is how Czech women became trapped in the double role of working full time and being completely responsible for running a household.

Czech women started to actively organize feminist groups in the 1990s. Their goals continue to be equal social and economic rights, as well as the right to be fully represented in government decisions about education, child care, maternity leave, and other family issues.

large portions of dumplings, buttered potatoes, or noodles topped with a thick sauce, and a heavily cooked vegetable such as sauerkraut or red cabbage. It was not unusual to start the meal with liver-dumpling or cabbage soup and top the whole thing off with coffee and a freshly baked poppy-seed pastry.

Similar eating habits still exist in the Czech Republic today, although many Czechs are picking up the trend of their European neighbors and becoming more calorie and cholesterol conscious.

Czech cuisine—although basically central European—has German, Hungarian, and Polish influences. Common flavorings are caraway seed, bacon, paprika, juniper berries, and a lot of salt.

Although supermarkets have become popular in Czech cities for their wide range of goods and lower prices, many older Czechs prefer the smaller family-owned shops that operate in older city neighborhoods. Shoppers stop almost daily on their way home from work for fresh meat, baked goods, and produce.

SPORTS AND RECREATION

Many Czechs make up for the calorie-rich foods they consume by maintaining a fairly active lifestyle. Czechs love nature and have a deep appreciation for their country's rivers, lakes, forests, and mountains. Whenever possible, city residents drive or take buses or bicycles to the countryside for weekends of camping, hiking, swimming, and in winter, skiing.

Children are encouraged at a very young age to participate in sports. They are traditionally given one week's vacation from school in February during which they are driven in groups to the mountains to ski. Children also go on school-sponsored overnight bicycling and canoeing trips.

Like most Europeans, Czechs love to watch sports like ice hockey, soccer, and tennis, and the country's athletes are some of the best in the world. Czechs are proud that their national ice hockey team has won the European title seventeen times, the world title six times, and it even won the 1998 Olympic gold

 ### SPORTS LEGEND EMIL ZÁTOPEK

Former Czech Olympian Emil Zátopek is considered a world-class athlete. In spite of his achievements, however, for many years his own country denied him the respect and admiration he deserved. Zátopek made his mark at the 1952 Olympic Games in Helsinki, where he won gold medals for the 5,000 meters, the 10,000 meters, and marathon races, all within eight days. He was honored throughout the world as an Olympic hero. After he returned to Czechoslovakia, he joined the army and became an active Communist Party member. He was one of many Czech Communists in the 1960s who believed in Alexander Dubcek's reforms. When the Soviets invaded Czechoslovakia in 1968 in an attempt to stop the Prague Spring, Zátopek publicly condemned the act. In spite of his status as sports icon, he was immediately expelled from both the army and the Communist Party and forced to work for almost ten years in Czechoslovakia's uranium mines. When he was finally released, he was hired by the government Ministry of Sport where he worked until his retirement in 1982. Emil Zátopek died in November 2000.

Ice hockey is a favorite sport in the Czech Republic. The Czech ice hockey team won the Olympic gold medal in 1998.

medal. Every major city has its own team and enthusiastic supporters. Individual ice-skating competitions are also popular because ice rinks are found all over the country, and almost everyone knows how to skate.

Another popular spectator sport in the Czech Republic is soccer, even though the national soccer team does not usually win as many titles as the hockey team does. Tennis is also very popular despite the fact that many of the most famous Czech tennis players (such as Ivan Lendl and Martina Navratilova) left their Czech homeland to become U.S. citizens. The Czech Tennis Open is held in Prague every April and is followed by tennis lovers throughout the world.

SURFING THE NET AND WATCHING TELEVISION

Not everyone in the Czech Republic is active or loves sports. Many enjoy more leisurely pursuits such as reading, personal

INVASION OF WESTERN POPULAR CULTURE

Before the Velvet Revolution of 1989, Czechs were forbidden access to many Western works of literature, art, and philosophy. When censorship was finally lifted, they were excited and eager to catch up on what they had missed. But it wasn't only serious culture they embraced. After so many drab years of state-controlled media and the scarcity of consumer goods, the Czechs delightedly imported all the Western pop culture they could, including punk rock, junk food, supermarkets, and American television. Free-market capitalism and the consumer goods made available meant visual displays of status. Sales of German luxury cars, Parisian fashions, and Japanese techno-toys skyrocketed. Prague rapidly became equally as fashionable as Paris.

Western-style advertising slogans quickly were incorporated into the Czech language. Today, English words and phrases such as *jeans, fitness, Internet, money-market, software, comeback,* and *homeless* are everyday words in Czech speech. Music fans use words like *jam session, rock, heavy metal,* and *blues.* Sometimes the words are adapted slightly. Young skateboardistas watch klips (music videos), listen to rapovani (rap music), and go to fitness-klubs. It's all Czech to them.

computing, and watching television. More and more Czech families have personal computers (PCs); Internet-based commerce and communication has become as popular as in Western countries. Parents and children alike spend a great deal of time playing computer games and surfing the Internet.

Another increasingly popular (and some critics say, mind-numbing) activity that Czech families engage in is watching television. Newspapers editorialize that the whole nation is watching too much junk, and legislators in parliament are debating ways to establish standards of broadcasting. This is a freedom-of-speech issue that has become controversial in a country that only too recently was repressed by rigid Communist censorship.

HOLIDAYS

A part of Czech family life that has remained consistent over the last one hundred years is the observation of religious holidays. Although many Czechs do not consider themselves especially religious, they still enthusiastically maintain holiday traditions, especially those centered around Christian religious holidays such as Easter and Christmas.

Easter is the most widely observed of all the holidays; preparations can start as early as February, depending when Easter

Sunday falls. The festivities start with a three-day feast called Shrovetide that immediately precedes Ash Wednesday. Ash Wednesday is the Christian day of atonement that begins forty days of Lenten fasting. Czechs observe Velikonoce, or Passion Week, starting on Palm Sunday and ending the following Easter Monday.

In addition to expressing the religious significance of the holiday, Czech Easter festivities, like those in many other parts of the world, incorporate a number of folk traditions left over from pre-Christian times. One is the hand painting of Easter eggs. The egg is an age-old symbol of life, and people believed its magical powers of fertility could be increased by decorating it with symbolic colors and designs. Each Czech region has developed its own secret dyeing techniques and distinctive patterns, which are passed along from generation to generation. These hand-painted Czech Easter eggs are treasured worldwide by collectors. In another old Czech Easter tradition, young boys with long willow wands chase girls. If a boy managed to tag a girl, she had to give him one of the Easter eggs she had painted.

Summer has its holidays, too, one Catholic, one Hussite. July 5 is Cyril and Methodius Day, which commemorates the arrival of Saints Cyril and Methodius, who brought Christianity to the Czech lands in the ninth century and developed the written Czech alphabet. The next day, July 6, commemorates the day the religious reformer Jan Hus was burned at the stake as a heretic in the fifteenth century.

Intricately painted Easter eggs are a Czech tradition.

Although more than 50 percent of Czechs claim to be nonreligious, a majority of them attend Midnight Mass on Christmas Eve every year. Christmas Eve, Christmas Day, and the ten days following are spent feasting and celebrating with family members. The Twelve Days of Christmas do not officially end until Tri Krale (Three Kings Day, or Epiphany) on January 6. This date commemorates the coming of the Magi to Bethlehem to bring gold, frankincense, and myrrh to the baby Jesus. It is not unusual for adults to dress up as kings that night and wander from pub to pub, singing Czech folk carols.

Another Czech tradition with Catholic religious roots is the celebration of Name Days. Many days of the year are marked by the celebration of a different Catholic saint. People named after saints are given flowers as presents each year to commemorate the day.

THE PLACE TO BE

Although the fall of Communism has brought changes to Czech life, Czechs themselves have managed to keep their identities. Keeping close family ties, getting a good education, and working to keep freedom and independence are all top priorities. But Czechs also enjoy socializing with friends over beer and good food and relaxing in the beautiful Czech countryside—just as they have been doing for countless centuries.

CZECH CULTURE

6

Czech lands have always been a great crossroads of ethnic groups, religious movements, and cultural ideas. It is only natural that Czech contributions to art, literature, and music have merged old and new, mixing Slavic with German and Austrian influences, sacred religious symbolism with sentimental folk themes, and classical art forms with cutting-edge, avant-garde ideas. This unique Czech identity is also reflected in the nation's architecture, industrial and scientific developments, and ongoing social contributions.

ARCHITECTURE

A visual representation of Czech identity is its urban architecture. Historians can only guess at what the earliest buildings in Bohemia and Moravia looked like. (They were constructed of wood and therefore did not survive.) By the ninth century the Slavic settlers who had migrated into Moravia from the east started building large but plain stone churches with thick walls and Romanesque (in the simple, classical style of the Romans) rotunda. Some of these churches are still standing today. But it wasn't until the twelfth century that other structures—bridges, castles, churches, monasteries, and merchants' homes—were also routinely built of stone. Amazingly, many of these structures are still in use today throughout the Czech Republic, especially in larger cities such as Prague.

Buildings erected in the thirteenth through sixteenth centuries were also constructed of stone, but the styles became much more elaborate and ornate. Architects began applying newly discovered scientific principles to building techniques. These new techniques created buildings with thinner walls, pointed arches, elaborately carved doorway columns, and great expanses of stained glass—without compromising the buildings' sturdiness. This style—known as Gothic—is some of the most stunning architecture in the Czech Republic today. Particularly

CZECH INVENTIONS

Czech artists have gained international reputations for their contributions to art, music, and literature. Less well known are the creative contributions of Czech inventors who have come up with such items as sugar cubes, contact lenses, and tubas.

Until the mid–nineteenth century, sugar came out of refineries molded into a solid cone shape. Housewives would hack chunks off the cone for their baking and other sweetening needs. Supposedly in the early 1840s the wife of a Czech sugary refinery owner named Jakub Rad nearly cut her finger off trying to saw sugar off a cone. Promising his wife he would find a solution, Rad invented a process to mold sugar into tiny cubes instead of large cones. In 1843 this so-called "Vienna sugar" made its debut appearance in Czech stores. The idea soon caught on around the world.

The combination of Czech inventiveness and industrial technology even changed the music business. In 1870 the internationally renowned composer Richard Wagner was writing the dramatic opera *Die Walkure* and needed an instrument no symphonies had: a musical horn that could produce a full, very deep sound. He commissioned Czech inventor Václav Cerveny to create one. Cerveny presented Wagner with a strange-looking tangle of brass tubing that he called a tuba. Wagner was delighted and the instrument has been used in bands and symphony orchestras ever since. Since then, the Cerveny family has become known as the manufacturer of the world's best tubas.

Otto Wichterle, a well-known inventor in post–World War II Czechoslovakia, thought of the idea of a plastic contact lens in 1957. After running a number of successful tests, he immediately saw the tremendous marketing potential of this cheap, easy-to-manufacture product. To prove it, he made a lens-casting machine using the motor from his record player. By 1962 he had sold more than five thousand lenses in the Czech Republic alone. At first his invention was scoffed at outside Czechoslovakia, but it caught on by the 1970s, especially in the United States.

The thousands of other inventions Czechs have given the world over the centuries include the mass production of beer, stereo sound technology, and boat propellers. The government patent office continues to receive more than eight hundred patent applications every year.

The sugar cube was invented in a sugar refinery in the Czech Republic.

The Saint Vitus Cathedral is a stunning example of Gothic architecture.

well known structures are the Saint Vitus Cathedral and the Old Town Bridge Tower of the famous Charles Bridge, both in the heart of Prague.

Sixteenth-century architects rebelled against the elaborate Gothic designs and sought instead the simple grace and symmetry that the Greeks and Romans had achieved with their temples and coliseums. These classical buildings became known as Renaissance architecture.

Architecture styles changed again in the seventeenth century. The Thirty Years' War, which ended in 1648, had devastated much of Europe. When the damaged buildings were rebuilt or replaced, architects added richly sculptured frescoes (huge murals) and elaborate gilded ornamentation. This Baroque style

Large murals and gilded ornamentation on the exterior of this Czech building characterize the Baroque style.

was particularly evident in large, expensive Catholic cathedrals intended to invoke an awe of God in parishioners. Over the course of the next one hundred years, architects tried to outdo each other, taking the Baroque style to an even more elaborate extreme. This style was known as Rococo.

At the beginning of the twentieth century Czech architects rebelled against the excesses of Rococo architecture and instead revived earlier, more classical styles. Over the next decades, strikingly elegant Art Deco buildings and other modern styles emerged. But after World War II, under the repressive influences of the totalitarian Communist regime, architecture became strictly functional and quite boring. Buildings erected from the 1950s through the 1980s were mostly massive, ugly housing projects and featureless, drab government buildings. Because much of the earlier, magnificently decorated architecture of Prague and other Czech cities did not match this austere new look, the Communist government ordered the facades (front or face) of many buildings to be plastered over. One of the first projects ordered by the new Czech government after the fall of Communism in 1989 was to slowly and systemically blast away the plasterwork to reveal the original architecture underneath.

PAINTING AND SCULPTURE

The painting and sculpture created by Czech artists over the centuries has usually included many of the same elements as the prevailing architectural styles. The earliest examples of Czech art, the painted frescoes or murals that adorned the inside stone walls of Romanesque churches, have religious and simple designs. The engineering technology developed in the thirteenth century allowed architects to incorporate massive windows, arches, and buttresses into their building designs. Artists immediately responded by creating masterpieces of stained glass for church and cathedral windows, and sculptors carved ornate images of biblical figures into the stone columns, arches, and buttresses.

During the Renaissance, churches and cathedrals added large, beautifully painted illuminations of the Bible and other religious works to decorate their walls and altars. Czech artists became so renowned for their painting expertise and techniques that hundreds of artists came from all over Europe to work and study in Bohemia. Prague was a thriving center of Western art during the Renaissance.

Although Czech artists were considered some of the best in Europe, Czech art during this time was not particularly unique. Czech art did not really come into its own until the late eighteenth and early nineteenth centuries, during the height of the Czech National Revival. Artists within the movement known as Czech Realism rendered detailed portrayals of everyday objects and scenes, traditional Czech dress and holiday traditions, and myths and legends from Czech folklore. Prominent Czech artists from this period include Antonín Machek, Václav Brozik, and Josef Manes. Czech artist, illustrator Alfons Mucha, became famous throughout Europe and the United States for his advertising posters.

As the Czech National Revival Movement grew, Czech artists experimented with new ideas and expanded their techniques.

ALFONS MUCHA

One of the Czech Republic's beloved artists, Alfons Mucha, was born in Bohemia in 1860 and moved to Paris thirty years later. It was there that he became known for creating advertising posters for the celebrated actress Sarah Bernhardt. His unique Art Nouveau style was characterized by twisting, swirling flower and hair motifs, and it set the standard for poster art.

After World War I Mucha returned to Czechoslovakia and organized a Slavic arts and crafts movement, which combined elements of Art Nouveau with classic national themes. He was also commissioned to design a series of postage stamps by the government when Czechoslovakia gained independence in 1918.

Mucha worked in many different genres. In addition to sculpture, commercial art, jewelry, interior decoration, and stage design, he experimented with lettering and calligraphy to produce original and often copied typefaces. He died in 1939.

Alfons Mucha is best known for his use of Art Nouveau style in his elaborate posters.

By the early decades of the twentieth century, Prague had become a major center of cutting-edge modern art. Avant-garde painters such as Anton Kosarek, Josef Čapek, and Emil Filla, and sculptors Otto Gutfreund and Nove Mesto, captured international attention by becoming major influences on the modern art movements that would follow.

Unfortunately, the freedom and independence that nurtured great art during this period was squashed when the Nazis invaded Czech lands in the 1930s. The repression continued during the forty-year Communist regime that followed. Czech art that was allowed to be produced during the 1950s and 1960s was, like the architecture of the period, functional but drab and boring. Almost all of it featured Communist themes about dedicating one's life to the good of the state.

Although Czech art did show signs of dissent and originality during the brief period of the Prague Spring in 1968, not until censorship was lifted after the Velvet Revolution of 1989 did

Czech artists again begin to push the limits of their creativity. Today Prague is again considered to be a leader of the world art scene with painters and sculptors such as Milena Dopitiva and Karel Pokorny, who use their art in often dramatic ways to express controversial social and political statements.

LITERATURE

Literature is another art form that has vividly reflected the cultural mix of Czech identity and its political struggles over the centuries. Almost all early literary works were either hymns or religious texts. In the thirteenth century, in addition to spending long hours copying the Bible and other religious texts, monks began writing down the Czech legends and history that had been previously passed from generation to generation only through oral storytelling. By the sixteenth century the monks had expanded their writings to include essays on morality and descriptions of daily life and travel to foreign lands.

The pope believed that these Czech writings were spreading non-Catholic ideas and were therefore dangerous. When he sent the Crusades to crush the Hussite movement, he also ordered that all books written in Czech be confiscated and burned. Czech literature and the Czech written language itself nearly ceased to exist. It was kept alive secretly in isolated villages by a few Czechs who knew how to read and write.

By the time the Austrian Habsburgs had firm control over their European empire in the eighteenth century, any literature produced in Czech lands was written in either German or Latin. As Czech scholars began rediscovering their heritage during the Czech National Revival Movement in the late 1880s, they became angry and frustrated that there were no accounts of their history written in their own language. They immediately set out to change that. One of the many writers of that period who revived the written Czech language and rediscovered Czech history was the poet Hynek Macha, whose famous poem *Maj* (May) came to symbolize the rejuvenating spring of the new movement. The Czech history and legends written during this period later inspired such international renowned poets as Jan Neruda and Svatopluk Cech, as well as Czech painters, sculptors, and composers.

Early-twentieth-century Czech writers, like their artist and architect counterparts, were at the forefront of literary styles and quickly attracted international attention. Perhaps one of the most well known was Franz Kafka. In a series of novels and

FRANZ KAFKA

The first sentence of Franz Kafka's most well known novel, *The Metamorphosis,* reveals its bizarre and unsettling nature: "As Gregor Samsa awoke one morning from uneasy dreams he found himself transformed in his bed into a gigantic insect." In *The Metamorphosis* and in his other works, Kafka created improbable but terrifying situations that served as metaphors for the horrors of modern life.

Kafka knew only too well what he was writing about. He was born in Prague in 1883 at a time when Czech nationalism was on the rise and many Czechs despised the German-dominated Habsburg empire in power. It was also a time when many Czech Catholics and Protestants openly despised Czech Jews. Kafka considered himself Czech, and like other Czechs, wanted his country to be free and independent. But because he was Jewish and spoke German rather than the Czech language the nationalists were trying to revive, Kafka faced constant discrimination.

When he was just sixteen, Kafka realized how dangerous Czech anti-Semitism was becoming. Outrageous rumors and stereotypes about Jews had been circulating through Prague for years. The rumor was that Jews were using Christian blood to prepare the special matzos (unleavened bread) for Passover. When a young Christian girl mysteriously turned up dead with her throat slit with a knife, it triggered anti-Semitic riots in Prague and throughout the rest of Bohemia. Within weeks massive boycotts were organized against Jewish-owned stores; many were ransacked and destroyed. That was when Kafka started writing.

Kafka earned a law degree, but took a clerical position at the Workers' Accident Insurance Institute. He never married and lived in his parents' house for most of his life. He was characterized by friends as being depressed and often obsessed about becoming ill. He died in 1924 of tuberculosis.

Other stories written by Franz Kafka include *The Trial, The Castle,* and "A Hunger Artist." Today he is considered an important member of the literary canon.

short stories, Kafka wrote about the meaningless violence and grotesque absurdity of modern life. In his story *The Metamorphosis,* the main character awakens one morning to find himself transformed into a giant, helpless cockroach who is shunned by his disgusted family until he dies in shame and loneliness. Kafka's stories made powerful statements about anti-Semitism, mass propaganda, and totalitarian governments. Even though Kafka died before the Nazis invaded Czechoslovakia, Hitler thought his work was so dangerous that he ordered many of Kafka's unpublished manuscripts destroyed and banned those already in print. A close friend of Kafka's managed to hide some of his unpublished work. It was not until the 1950s that his books were again made available.

Many other great twentieth-century Czech writers have made controversial political and social statements through their work. Karel Čapek was a human-rights activist who wrote about the horrors of World War I and also wrote futuristic fiction. In one of his science fiction novels he coined the word *robot*, now used around the world.

During the years of Soviet censorship following World War I, the only Czech writers who became known were those who wrote Communist-approved literature. Not until the Prague Spring of the late 1960s did a new generation of writers begin to make their voices heard. However, when this brief period of artistic freedom ended abruptly with the invasion of Soviet armies, the majority of the most important authors of the generation were exiled and forced to continue their work abroad. For the next two decades their works circulated in Czech lands only in typed copies. Among these writers were Milan Kundera, Arnost Lustig, Egon Hostovsky, and Josef Skvorecky. Kundera is best known for his novel *The Incredible Lightness of Being*, which examined a love story set against the pain and terror of living under a totalitarian government. In 1988 the book was made into a movie. It gained immediate international popularity and was nominated for several Academy Awards. In 1984 Jaroslav Seifert, who wrote about similar themes, became the first Czech writer to be awarded the Nobel Prize for literature.

Franz Kafka's literary works revealed his anguish about modern life.

MUSIC

Music has also played an important role in defining Czech identity both at home and abroad. Czech musical history dates back to the religious hymns and Gregorian chants of the Middle Ages. By the seventeenth century Prague had become an important cultural center of Europe and was renowned for its classical symphonic and chamber music. Between 1583 and 1612, Habsburg king Rudolf II founded the Imperial Orchestra of Prague, one of the biggest symphonies in Europe. He actively sponsored Czech composer J. D. Zelenka, who was hailed as one of the leading composers of the age. By the end of the eighteenth century the elite of Europe were mad about opera. Prague, with its several municipal opera houses, became opera's center stage. It was here that some of composer Wolfgang Mozart's famous operas had their opening nights. The Czech Philharmonic Orchestra was founded in 1896 and is still considered one of the world's premier symphony orchestras.

The country's passion for music produced many world-renowned classical composers, including Bedřich Smetana (1824–1884), known for his symphonies and operas such as *The Bartered Bride*, and Antonín Dvořák (1841–1904), who has been particularly celebrated for his chamber music, symphonies, and concertos. Like many other Czech artists and musicians, both were passionate not just about their music, but also about their love of country and their identity as Czechs. They frequently incorporated Czech folk melodies into their pieces and wrote about the beauty of their Czech homeland. Their music is still played by symphonies throughout the world.

Nineteenth-century Czech music did not consist solely of serious opera and classical symphonic pieces. Czechs have always loved to dance and the Revival Movement brought back many danceable folk tunes. Despite the widespread belief that the polka originated in Poland, it is in fact a Czech folk dance. Several versions of the polka (such as the polka waltz and the polka mazurka) became popular after 1840, not only in Europe but in the United States as well. Smetana wrote many popular polkas for the Czechs, but the tune most Americans would instantly recognize, the "Beer Barrel Polka," was written by a lesser-known Czech composer named Jaromir Vejdova.

Not even Communism could repress the underground jazz and rock music that developed in Czechoslovakia in the 1950s, although punishment for those even listening to the music, let alone playing or composing it, could be severe. Underground clubs and alternative theaters became musical hotbeds that fostered the creative efforts of world-famous musicians such as Jiri Stivin and Rudolf Dasek. Some musicians fled Czechoslovakia to work abroad. Keyboardist Jan Hamr, who escaped to the United States in the 1970s, became an American jazz-rock star named Jan Hammer. Since the Velvet Revolution, the Czech jazz scene has grown considerably, especially in Prague.

THEATER

Theater has always played a vital role in developing a national sense of Czech identity and promoting the struggle for freedom. It has also worked to keep the Czech language alive.

The Czech theater tradition started in the seventeenth century with puppet shows. The theater companies first traveled from place to place, but the shows were so popular, especially with adults, that Prague and other large cities erected special theater houses for the expensively staged productions. The large marionette puppets used in everything from Shakespearean plays to fairy tales were works of art themselves: beautifully carved, painted, and costumed. Today, puppet shows staged in Prague's Theater of Spejbl and Hurvinek entertain audiences from all over the world. Large and expensive wooden puppets are sold as souvenirs.

Václav Havel was a popular playwright before he became president of the Czech Republic.

Regular theater productions (with human actors) became an important part of the Czech National Revival Movement of the 1800s.The first permanent Czech theater opened in Prague in 1862 with plays about Czech social and political history, performed not in the German language of the reigning Habsburg empire but in the Czech language. The theater became so popular and so influential in reviving the Czech people's interest in their own cultural history that it has remained a symbol of Czech Revivalism ever since. It also pushed twentieth-century censorship to its limits by staging comedies and musical revues that satirized Fascism and Communism.

Playwrights and actors who staged nationalist plays often risked prison and even death for doing so, but their daring and their art helped keep the spirit of Czech independence and resistance alive. Many of the Czech Republic's political activists started as playwrights and poets. Václav Havel, the country's famous dissident playwright, went on to become the new Czech Republic's first president. His plays continue to be translated and performed all over the world.

FILM

Film is yet another form of twentieth-century Czech cultural expression. The first Czech film was produced in 1898 by director Jan Krizenecky. Movie theaters started operating in Prague as early as 1907. In the 1930s Czech writers and cinematographers received international awards and recognition for their exceptionally produced artistic films and documentaries. They were the first to produce newsreels with sound. After World War II, when the Communists nationalized the Czech film industry, creative expression was harshly censored and most Czech films became little more than propaganda. During that time only politically harmless Czech puppet films and cartoons for children achieved any worldwide recognition for artistic achievement.

It was not until the late 1960s, when Czech culture was enjoying its Prague Spring, that a new generation of cinematographers started taking creative chances again. Politically controversial films from that period such as *The Shop on Main Street* immediately caught the attention of moviegoers in the West and received numerous international awards. The depiction of life under Communism, however, angered Soviet leaders. After the Soviets invaded Czechoslovakia in 1968, the films were banned and the producers prohibited from making any others.

When the Czechs won their independence in 1989 the government privatized the film industry and lifted political censorship. Today, Czech film has regained the international status it once enjoyed. Two important annual film festivals are held in the Czech Republic: the International Film Festival in Karlovy Vary and the Children's Film Festival in Zlín.

Two highly regarded Czech directors are Milos Forman and Jiri Menzel, whose films are played in movie houses all over the world. Forman won an Oscar for his films *One Flew Over the Cuckoo's Nest* and *Amadeus,* while Menzel received an Oscar for *Closely Watched Trains.*

FOLK ART

Folk culture is defined as the local crafts, music, and traditional dress developed over hundreds of years by people in rural villages and farming communities. Czech folk culture is particularly rich because Bohemia and Moravia were at the crossroads of European trade and were therefore influenced by many other cultures, especially German, Hungarian, and Slavic. Czech folk culture reached its high point from the mid–eighteenth to the mid–nineteenth centuries.

The traditional folk costumes worn by men and women for special occasions such as weddings and religious holidays were intricately embroidered with geometric patterns, primarily in

black, red, gold, and blue. The men wore square-cut white shirts under red vests with black trousers, while the women traditionally wore white blouses with puffed, gathered sleeves, black embroidered aprons over white pleated skirts, and large, brightly painted red scarves. The color combinations and the designs of the embroidery were unique to each Czech region.

The Czechs value richly painted designs on their chinaware.

Czechs decorated more than just their clothing with bright colors and geometric designs. Household possessions such as furniture, dishes, utensils, and containers were also brightly painted and/or ornately carved. Bohemians became famous for their beautiful hand-blown crystal glassware, often decorated with gold foil; Moravians were known for their richly painted, delicate chinaware. Both wood and stone were also carved and brightly painted. In addition to decorating useful, everyday household items, Czechs created folk art for its own sake in the form of small sculptures and paintings. The most popular subjects were saints and other religious figures or scenes from nature. Many people painted scenes on homemade glass squares, then framed them and hung them in a window or on a wall.

Many Czech men were talented woodcarvers who carved and painted wooden puppets, dolls, and other toys for their children and grandchildren. They also painted and carved commemorative gifts for special occasions such as weddings, births, and religious holidays. Today, hand-carved Czech nativity scenes and hand-painted Easter eggs are valued by collectors throughout the world.

However they choose to express their heritage, whether through literature or music, art or architecture, the Czech people have much to celebrate. Their rich cultural contributions are a vibrant reflection of how people in Czech lands have celebrated their families, traditions, and beliefs over the centuries. But more than that, they are a reflection of the Czech spirit itself: enduring and indomitable.

EPILOGUE

INTO TOMORROW

As the Czech Republic enters the first few years of the new millennium, it faces numerous challenges. The transition from Communist satellite to independent republic has been challenging and often overwhelming; a struggling economy, often strained relations with European neighbors, and internal problems such as crime and pollution constantly present problems a new democracy has had little experience with. Even so, Czechs are proud to be controlling their own destiny at last. And they're learning fast.

PROBLEMS FACING A NEW FREE-MARKET ECONOMY

Reorienting the economy toward free-market capitalism has been difficult and complicated. To make the changeover, the Czech Republic has had to privatize, or turn over to private ownership, the businesses and industries formerly run by the Communist government. The country has also needed to modernize its banking system, develop a securities and exchange commission to regulate its new stock market, establish guidelines for regulating energy use and telecommunications, and revamp its entire legal system. Today, more than 85 percent of the country's enterprises are privately owned and operated, although the government still controls most of the banking and much of the country's energy, transportation, and communications enterprises.

In the early 1990s Western investors predicted that the Czech economy would quickly become prosperous and invested heavily in privatized Czech industry. But by 1997 rising inflation and unemployment problems, turmoil within the country's political parties, and scandals over the corruption involved in some of the privatizing scared away foreign investors. By the end of the decade the Czech Republic was undergoing a recession so severe that banks collapsed because of mismanagement and because they were unable to collect on loans they had made to unsuccessful privatization enterprises.

To make matters even more complicated, so many political parties were vying for power in the Czech Republic that no one party ever achieved a clear-cut majority. Because each party had its own ideas about how the country's economic problems should be solved, every piece of legislation took a long time to pass—if it passed at all. Fears about the economy made Czech people impatient and dissatisfied with the government representatives they had elected, even though many of these elected officials had been the revolutionary leaders who had helped foment the Velvet Revolution. By the year 2000 President Václav Havel was still well liked and respected by governments throughout the West for his revolutionary passion and integrity, yet he was rapidly losing the affection and respect of his own people. After the economy finally started turning around again, polls indicated that many Czechs remained dissatisfied with their leaders.

COURTING INTERNATIONAL INVESTMENT

Foreign investment is a vital tool in bringing Czech industry into the twenty-first century. The United States is the third-largest investor in the Czech Republic, behind Germany and the Netherlands. More than fifty thousand foreign-owned or partly foreign owned companies are registered in the Czech Republic, including major multinational corporations such as Philip Morris, Ford, Conoco Oil, Volkswagen, Procter & Gamble, and Pepsi-Cola, among others. In 1999 the amount of foreign investment more than doubled to $5 billion. The Czech Republic has created a number of important new incentives for foreign investors: waving of taxes for ten years, no customs duty for imports of modern technology and equipment, and subsidies for retraining Czech workers for high-tech jobs.

Imports of all kinds are integral to the Czech economy. Besides finished consumer goods, the Czech Republic imports a tremendous amount of transportation equipment, specialized machine tools, chemicals, fuel, and raw materials from the United States, as well as manufactured items such as cars and appliances. (Total trade between the United States and the Czech Republic equaled $1.6 billion in 1998.) Newly privatized Czech businesses are also offering incentives to people to move to the Czech Republic with their special consulting, marketing, public relations, telecommunications, and/or financing skills.

TAKING A PLACE ON THE WORLD STAGE

Facilitating trade relations is an important reason for joining international organizations, which is why the Czech Republic has worked hard for several years to comply with the entry requirements for joining the European Union (EU). But trade is certainly not the only reason for membership in international organizations, especially given its history of being the strategic football of its power-hungry neighbors. The Czech Republic became a member of the Organization for Economic Cooperation and Development (OECD) in 1995 and, in 1999, the North Atlantic Treaty Organization (NATO). As a NATO member, the Czech Republic contributes to the alliance's strategy defense pact, defending it in part from the Eastern bloc the country was once a part of.

As a member of the United Nations, the Czech Republic contributes forces to UN peacekeeping missions. The country allows

The Czech Republic has experienced tremendous growth and a strengthened economy as a result of foreign investment.

NATO to use its airspace and airports and has offered humanitarian relief in the form of medical care and political refuge. Czech politicians have also been outspoken in joining other nations in condemning the actions of dictators such as Yugoslavia's Slobodan Milošević, Iraq's Saddam Hussein, and Cuba's Fidel Castro.

OTHER PROBLEMS AT HOME

International relations and a struggling economy are not the only events that make Czech headlines. Two of the biggest issues are crime and racism.

The crime rate in Czechoslovakia before 1989 was relatively low because the same police state that severely restricted political freedom also deterred criminal activity. People suspected of anti-Communist thought or action were banned from working in their professions, imprisoned, or sometimes they simply disappeared. There was no due process of law, no guarantee of basic human rights. Crimes such as murder or theft usually received harsh punishment. As a result, even the nonpolitical crime rate was relatively low.

When the Velvet Revolution in 1989 outlawed the police state and guaranteed freedom of speech and other human rights, the rate of political crimes dropped almost to zero. But since then, the crime rate in general has increased dramatically and the Czech government has been working hard to implement a plan to contain it.

There are many reasons for the soaring crime rate. Although the economy is finally starting to turn around, unemployment is still relatively high. Unable to find work, some people have turned to picking pockets and stealing cars. Access to guns is easy, which has doubled the rate of murder and other violent crime. Drugs—under the control of organized crime—have become widespread. Privatization of business and industry has also led to a large increase in white-collar crimes such as fraud, political corruption, and tax evasion. The increase in sex crimes, especially child and teenage prostitution, is alarming. One of the first agendas for the new Czech parliament was to pass new laws to prosecute criminals, to train new law enforcement agencies, and to create an adequate court system to process criminals.

RACISM

By restricting freedom of speech, the Communists restricted hate crimes and discrimination that have erupted since they lost power. Racism toward religious and ethnic minorities has existed in Czech lands for centuries. But when Communist control ended in 1989, racism, especially against Romany, Jewish, and Vietnamese Czechs, erupted in frighteningly vocal and violent ways. The new Czech government has passed legislation against hate crimes, but as in all democracies, freedom of speech often makes verbal racist attacks difficult to prosecute. A growing number of neo-Nazi skinheads and other white supremacy groups have taken the attacks beyond name-calling and vandalism to terrorist tactics that include rape and murder.

In spite of the increasingly violent racism, minorities have pushed for an end to economic discrimination. The more militant minorities become in their demands for equal pay and the elimination of job discrimination, the more they seem to provoke even more racism, especially among unemployed Czechs in the majority who need a scapegoat for their economic difficulties.

Skinheads clash with police and other protesters at a rally at Old Town Square in Prague in 1994.

Czech problems, whether local, national, or international, are not so different from those in any other Western democracy. In fact, considering that the country is little more than a decade old and its people have had to make all the major changes that come with a transition from totalitarianism to democracy, from government control of business to free-market capitalism, they deserve a lot of credit. They have come a long way in a very short period of time. There is every reason to believe that in the years to come, they will travel much, much further.

Facts About Czech Republic

Government

Official name: Czech Republic (Česka Republika)

Government type: Parliamentary democracy

Administrative divisions: 73 districts

Independence: January 1, 1993 (Czechoslovakia split into the Czech and Slovak Republics)

Executive branch: President Václav Havel (since February 2, 1993); Prime Minister Milos Zeman (since July 17, 1998)

Legislative branch: Bicameral (two house) Parliament; Senat (81 seats elected by popular vote); Poslanecka Snemovna (200 seats elected by popular vote)

Elections: President, elected by Parliament every five years, next in January 2003; Senat, staggered two-, four-, and six-year terms; Poslanecka Snemova, every four years, next in June 2002

People

Population: 10,272,179 (July 2000 est.)

Population growth: -0.08 percent (2000 est.)

Birth rate: 9.1 birth/1,000 population

Death rate: 10.87 deaths/1,000 population

Infant mortality: 5.63 deaths/1,000 live births

Life expectancy at birth: males, 71.01 years; females, 78.22 years

Ethnic groups: Czech, 81.2 percent; Moravian, 13.2 percent; Slovak, 3.1 percent (March 1991)

Religions: None (atheist), 39.8 percent; Roman Catholic, 39.2 percent; Protestant, 4.6 percent; Orthodox, 3 percent; other, 13.4 percent

Official language: Czech

Literacy: 99.9 percent (1999 est.)

Geography

Area: 31,546 square miles (78,866 sq. km.)

Capital city: Prague (population, 1,213,800)

Boundaries: Austria, Germany, Poland, Slovakia

99

Terrain: Bohemia in the west consists of rolling plains, hills, and plateaus surrounded by low mountains; Moravia in the east consists of very hilly country.

Natural resources: hard coal, soft coal, kaolin, clay, graphite, timber

Land use: arable land, 41 percent; forests and woodland, 34 percent; permenent pastures, 11 percent; permanent crops, 2 percent; other, 12 percent (1993 est.)

ECONOMY

Monetary unit: Czech koruna (Kc)

All the following monetary figures are in U.S. dollars.

Exchange rate: 35.63 Kc= $1

Gross domestic product: $120.8 billion (1999 est.); agriculture contributes 5 percent to the economy; industry, 42 percent; services, 53 percent

Annual per capita income: $11,700 (1999 est.)

Labor force: 5.203 million (1999 est.); 32 percent work in industry; 5.6 percent in agriculture; 8.7 percent in consruction; 6.9 percent in transport and communications; 46.8 percent in services

Unemployment rate: 9 percent (1999 est.)

Budget: revenues, $16.4 billion; expenditures, $17.3 billion

Industries: fuels, ferrous metallurgy, machinery and equipment, coal, motor vehicles, glass, armaments

Agricultural products: grains, potatoes, sugar beets, hops, fruit; pigs, cattle, poultry

Exports: $26.9 billion (1999); main exports are machinery and transport equipment, 41 percent; other manufactured goods, 40 percent; chemicals, 8 percent; raw materials and fuel, 7 percent

Imports: $29 billion (1999); main imports are machinery and transport equipment, 39 percent; other manufactured goods, 21 percent; chemicals, 12 percent; raw materials and fuel, 10 percent; food, 5 percent

NOTES

CHAPTER 1: GEOGRAPHY

1. Kosmas of Prague, "Chronica Boemorum" (*Czech chronicle*). www.uni-jena.de/~x7scre/Czech%20Republic.html

CHAPTER 3: FIRST STIRRINGS OF NATIONALISM

2. Woodrow Wilson, "Speech on the Fourteen Points," *Congressional Record*, 65th Cong., 2nd sess., 1918, pp. 680–81.

CHAPTER 4: COMMUNIST CONTROL

3. Paul Halsall, "The Warsaw Pact, 1955." www.fordham.edu/halsall/mod/1955warsawpact.html

4. Quoted in Josef Korbel, *Twentieth Century Czechoslovakia: The Meanings of Its History*. New York: Columbia University Press, 1977, p. 230.

5. Radio Prague Online, "The Velvet Revolution." www.radio.cz/history/history15.html

CHRONOLOGY

300 B.C.
Celts settle in Bohemia

A.D. 450
Huns and other Slavs migrate west into Bohemia and Moravia

830–906
Great Moravian empire rules Czech lands

906–1306
Přemsylid dynasty is founded

1419
First Defenestration of Prague and beginning of fifteen-year
Hussite Wars

1526–1914
Czech lands become part of the Habsburg empire

1618
Protestant uprising and start of Thirty Years' War

1620
Protestant Czechs defeated at Battle of White Mountain

1850–1900
National Revival Movement of Czech identity and nationalism

1914–1918
World War I; Czechs and Slovaks gain international support
for independence

1918
Habsburg empire defeated; independent Czechoslovakia
created

1938
Munich Pact forces Czechslovakia to give up Sudetenland to
Nazi Germany

1939
Hitler invades and occupies rest of Czechoslovakia

1945
Czechoslovakia liberated by Allied forces; beginning of Soviet occupation

1968
Prague Spring crushed by invading Soviet troops

1977
Dissident Václav Havel forms Charter 77 to protest Communist rule

1989
Bloodless Velvet Revolution overthrows Communists; Havel becomes president

1990
Free elections held; parliamentary government established

1991
Privatization of state-run agriculture and industry begins

1992
Czechoslovakia splits into the separate nations of the Czech Republic and Slovakia

1995
Czech Republic becomes a member of NATO

Suggestions for Further Reading

Books

Vladimir Brych and Jirini Langhammerova, *A Thousand Years of Czech Culture: Riches from the National Museum in Prague.* Winston-Salem, NC: Old Salem Press Distributed by University of Washington Press, 1996. A pictorial respresentation of a 1996 art exhibit that included more than two hundred historic Czech artifacts and works of art, examining Czech politics, religion, folk customs, and decorative and fine arts, as well as music and theater from the sixth century to the present.

Steven Otfinoski, *The Czech Republic.* New York: Facts On File, 1997. A description of the Czech struggle to establish democracy and a free-market economy after decades of Communist rule.

Efstathia Sioras, *Czech Republic.* New York: Marshall Cavendish, 1999. A book for young adult readers about the history and culture of the Czech Republic.

Hana Volavkova, ed., *I Never Saw Another Butterfly.* Children's Drawings and Poems from Theresienstadt Concentration Camp, 1942–1944. Trans. Jeanne Nemcová. New York: McGraw-Hill, 1964. Moving poems and pictures created by children who were interred in the Terezin Nazi Concentration Camp in Czechosolvakia during World War II. Fewer than one hundred of the fifteen thousand children survived.

Websites

www.ctknews.com. "Czech Happenings"—a news update in English of Czech events, including sports, art, literature, and photographs of Prague.

www.czechstore.com/czechonline. Read about Czech government, culture, economics; listen to the Czech national anthem and to live Czech radio; chat with other people about travel to the Czech Republic.

www.ecn.cz/cmvu/. Czech Museum of Fine Arts online.

www.locallingo.com. Czech language lessons, Czech recipes, and examples of Czech art and music.

www.lonelyplanet.com/dest/eur/cze.htm. An overview of travel through the Czech Republic.

www.privat.schlund.de/Halamicek/1968/. Photographs documenting the 1968 invasion of Czechoslovakia.

www.radio.cz/english. Radio Prague Online in an English translation.

WORKS CONSULTED

Peter Demetz, *Prague in Black and Gold: Scenes from the Life of a European City*. New York: Hill and Wang, 1997. A book about the cultural forces that shaped the history of the Czech capital, Prague, written by a Yale literary professor who left Prague as a young man in 1949.

Eda Kriseová, *Václav Havel: The Authorized Biography*. Trans. Caleb Crain. New York: St. Martin's Press, 1993. The life of Czech president Václav Havel, focusing primarily on his role as playwright and revolutionary in the 1980s.

Josef Macek, *The Hussite Movement in Bohemia*. Trans. Vilém Fried and Ian Milner. London: Lawrence and Wishart, 1965. A history of the Hussite religious revolution in Czech lands in the fifteenth century.

Jan Novak, *Commies, Crooks, Gypsies, Spooks and Poets: Thirteen Books of Prague in the Year of the Great Lice Epidemic*. S. Royalton, VT: Steerforth Press, 1995. A witty memoir about growing up in Czechoslovakia during (and after) Communist rule.

Elizabeth Pond, *The Rebirth of Europe*. Washington, DC: Brookings Institution Press, 1999. A history of the economic and political development of Europe since World War II, including Czech involvement in NATO and the European Union (EU).

Derek Sayer, *The Coasts of Bohemia: a Czech History*. Trans. Alena Sayer. Princeton, NJ: Princeton University Press, 1998. A vivid social and cultural history of the Czech Republic by a Canadian sociologist.

INDEX

107

PICTURE CREDITS

Cover photo: Uniphoto, Inc.
Archive Photos, 27, 28, 33, 34, 36, 58, 59, 80, 87
Archive Photos/Hulton Getty, 38, 46, 47
Archive Photos/Sheila Masson, 81, 82
Archive Photos/Reuters, 64, 75, 97
Corbis, 12, 31
Corbis/Archivo Iconografico, 26, 30
Corbis/Betmann, 77
Corbis/Christie's Images, 84
Corbis/Owen Franken, 65
Corbis/Martin Jones, 11
Corbis/Barry Lewis, 71, 95
Corbis/David and Peter Turnley, 89
Corbis/Miroslav Zaji, 56, 60
FPG Int'l, 41, 53, 54
FPG Int'l/Farrell Grehan, 13
FPG Int'l/Al Michaud, 68
FPG Int'l/Vladimir Pcholkin, 18, 69
FPG Int'l/Telegraph Colour Library, 14, 17
FPG Int'l/David Wade, 91
Library of Congress, 23, 44
Stock Montage, 24, 35, 39, 42

ABOUT THE AUTHOR

Petra Press writes non-fiction for children and young adults, vidio scripts, and TV documentaries. Some of her most recent projects include books on settling the United States, Native American peoples, recent immigrants to the United States, and AIDS.